with love

Chasing Rainbows

G E Larrisey

First published by Lulu.com 30/10/2015.

ISBN: 978-1-326-21603-0

Front cover photography taken in Porthmadog 2015
Copyright © Ron and Gaynor Troake 20015.

Bible Verses Holy Bible, New International Version®, NIV®
Copyright ©1973, 1978, 1984, 2011

Sue Pinnick – editing.
Simon Peters and Mark Lewis - technical support.

Some names have been changed to protect identities and privacy.

Dedication

Dedicated to our very special son - the chickpea, without him, we would not have this story.

For Helen Wade - 'the most excited,' for her friendship, enthusiasm and support.

For Elaine Banks B.E.M - who always goes the extra mile.

And I would like to dedicate this story to each and everyone at Ferries Family Groups, and all the special needs parents that have come in to in our lives.

For you guys.

Psalm 139: 13, 14
For you created my inmost being;
You knit me together in my mother's womb.
I praise you because I am fearfully and wonderfully made;
Your works are wonderful,
I know that full well.

Contents

Foreword

There are millions of families out there struggling with children with special needs, fighting for support, fighting to be heard, but unless you have a child with special needs, you can never appreciate the stress and the daily struggle that these families endure. Our story is just one story. There are many different stories waiting to be told. There are different levels of special needs, some children needing a lot more care and support than others; however, we are all going through our own daily struggles that are unique to us.

I would never have known the world I was plummeted into if it hadn't been for one special little boy - a special little boy with special needs. We always knew that there was something different, but we couldn't quite put our finger on it. I suppose I was probably one of those ignorant people who had no clue about autism, until it happened to us. So, I would like to tell you our son's story and how we fought to get him the support that he needed. I hope to raise awareness by telling our story and also to inspire those going through the system that there is light at the end of the tunnel. Just knowing that you are not alone can be of great comfort. I don't profess to be some sort of expert; however, I am the expert of my own child.

The relevance of the chapter 'The letters' may not be apparent at first, in fact, there are two reasons why the letters are relevant. The first being, I had talked about our son in these letters and from them you can picture the quirky, funny little guy that he is. The second reason I will not divulge at this stage, but I will leave you to read on and work out their relevance later on.

I would also like to point out that the SEND code of practice has now been changed as from September 1st 2014. The process that

I went through and have written about here would be slightly different to the process one would go through now.

The Chickpea

I always seem to have a story to tell. Sometimes I don't stop for breath. I usually start with, "I'll try and cut this short." It never happens! I could talk the head off a pint.

I have lived a colourful life up until now and my latest story will be no exception. In order to tell my latest story I need to go back to the beginning and start with one I have already told previously, the story of the pregnancy and birth of my little boy. Because after all, that amongst other things is what my story is all about. I always refer to him as the chickpea (as all my friends know) so here I will use this same term.

It was a cold January in 2005. My husband and I, along with his Dad, went along to the motor cycle show in Manchester. As bikes and modified cars were a huge interest of ours we had been to the annual show a few times before. This year I felt a bit off though.

I remember commenting to my husband's Dad that I felt 'a bit rubbish' and he had replied, "Your not pregnant are ya G?"

Of course I wasn't!

I tried to enjoy the show and remedied this by buying a most expensive pair of hot pink and steel new rock boots, *as you do.*

Back at home and later in the week, it really started to bother me that my monthly curse was late by five days. I had never been this late before, not unless I had been pregnant. But there was no way I could be pregnant as I'd had the coil for five years. I had thought my missed period was something to do with my thyroid condition. It didn't even occur to me that I could actually be pregnant.

In January 2005 I did a pregnancy test just to rule it out. It showed positive but it wasn't very clear and my mind still couldn't settle so I asked my husband to bring home another one from work.

I recall saying to him, "pick up one of those expensive blue ones which will be clearer." I nearly fell off the toilet seat when it showed up pregnant straight away. How could I be? I still had the coil fitted!

The strange thing was I had been to the clinic earlier that week to have it removed as it was causing me a few problems. My husband and I had discussed trying for a baby in the near future as we were settled now. I had decided on taking the contraceptive pill instead for the time being. There was an hour long wait at the clinic so I had ended up having to leave before I was seen as I had to get back for the children coming home from school. I was going to go back another time.

My third test at the doctors confirmed my pregnancy and I cried with happiness. I was well chuffed and I thought, 'this is definitely meant to be.'

A few weeks in to my pregnancy I started to bleed and have abdominal pain. I was admitted to hospital on a Friday to await a scan. I worried that the coil was damaging my baby or I was going to miscarry because of it. I had to wait all weekend as the scan unit was not open until the Monday. So, I had the scan two days later which showed the amniotic sack but the doctor said she couldn't see my baby. I craned my neck to look at the screen, willing my infinitesimal life form to appear there and relieve us all. All I saw was the black dot the doctor had been referring to. I had drunk lots of water before the scan and I was desperate for the loo by now. I couldn't go. I was petrified of letting go and the nerves had overtaken my body. I shook like an autumn leaf and thought to myself, 'they're going to have to operate now to extract my wee.'

Another of several blood tests came back and the doctors said they could not confirm that I was still pregnant. The hormones in my blood were not doubling up the way they should have been and this was worrying. My husband and I were in bits at this point. We were just not getting any answers. It was decided that whether I was still pregnant or not my coil had to be removed. If I was still pregnant then it could cause a miscarriage anyway so I was more at risk leaving it where it was. Just as I made the decision to go ahead and have it removed the doctor came rushing in saying there had been a mistake with my blood tests and she had been looking at the wrong one. We gasped in anticipation. The latest test which she had now found, confirmed that I was definitely still pregnant. We cried with relief. Now all I had to do was hope that I didn't miscarry after the coil was removed. I was kept in hospital over night just in case, and I swore to high heaven I would never ever have the coil fitted again. The next day all my pain had completely vanished and I felt fine. It seems that my body had been trying to reject the coil and now that it was gone my pregnancy could progress normally, or so we thought.

At my routine twenty week scan an abnormality was detected. My baby's kidneys were dilated and swollen which signified a blockage of some sort. It was thought to be a condition called *renal valves*, or *posterior urethral valves*. Water was not able to pass out properly because of the blockage causing a back log of fluid into our baby's kidneys and bladder, in turn causing them to swell. I had to go to the hospital for regular scans from then on. There was talk of delivering the baby early if need be or operating through me to release some of the fluid pressure from his kidneys.

In June at twenty nine weeks pregnant I had another appointment at the hospital. After being left sitting in a hot, sweaty room for forty minutes with no air conditioning, the doctor finally arrived. I was feeling quite agitated by then anyway, wondering why no one had even popped their head in to see if we were OK or if we needed anything. There were plenty of staff members hovering around the reception desk, I had mentally noted. We were then told that our baby probably had downs syndrome as renal valves were associated with it. She said I could consider other options available to me, options meaning termination or adoption? I was horrified. I knew what the doctor was suggesting but I couldn't quite take it in. I was still trying to take in the fact that my baby could have downs syndrome.

I asked her, "what do you mean; I'm twenty nine weeks pregnant?"

Her answer was, "well in your case we would make an exception."

At twenty nine weeks? No way. I couldn't believe what I was hearing.

She was quite persistent and seemed to pressure me for an answer there and then. She asked me would I like some information on downs syndrome *if* I was going to keep the baby. I couldn't think straight. Of course I was going to keep my baby boy. No question. I could feel him kicking inside me. I'd already named him and I chatted to him when I was in the bath and watched his movements ripple across my bare belly. She waffled on a while longer to my husband. Everything she said to us was like a distant murmur to me. My head was buzzing and the room was still so hot and stuffy. I had to get out of there. I got up and ran from the room; floods of tears were blinding me. I just needed to go home and be with my family. It was my daughters fourteenth birthday that same day and I had organised a party for her for when we got back from the hospital. I had to get home for her. I had to put on a brave face, light the candles on her birthday cake and try to put things to the back of my mind. I greeted the guests and sat in the garden whilst my daughter opened her presents. She was blissfully unaware of our plight, as was everyone else.

It was a blur for a few days after that and I sunk in to a depression. I lay on the couch curled up trying to make head and tail of what was happening. I could feel my baby somersaulting inside me and moving about. I had already named him and loved him. He was part of me and my husband. How could the doctor have suggested I terminate his life at this late stage? If he did have downs we would cross that bridge when we came to it. He would still be our baby no matter what. I couldn't rest.

I eventually telephoned the hospital and told them what had happened at my appointment and I was put on to the specialist doctor. The doctor put my mind at ease after days of worry by telling me it was <u>not</u> likely that our baby had downs syndrome and we shouldn't have been told that. Although renal valves can be associated with downs syndrome, it was more likely <u>not</u> the case in our case. He explained that our baby probably had a little blockage in his doo dah so that when he had a wee it was rather like when you push against a door to open it, when you let go of the door, it swings back the other way. So much urine was passing through but then the door (flaps of skin inside the urethra) swings back the other way causing *'reflux'* or urine to go back up the wrong way, thus swelling his kidneys. Now that made sense to me.

The doctor (who turned out to be a junior doctor) we had seen on our last visit had been somewhat insensitive in her explanation. I felt relieved after this latest explanation. Not totally, but enough to carry on with hope. The remainder of my pregnancy was fraught with teenage shenanigans from my eldest two children.

On the 15h September 2005 I went in to labour. My husband rang work and told them he wouldn't be coming in that day. I stayed in bed all day listening to Chicago and Phantom of the Opera amidst my contractions. It relaxed me. Eventually when the pain began to get too much I knew it was time to go to the hospital. At one point I thought I was going to give birth in the car. Every bump in the road seemed to bring the contractions on stronger and I winced with pain. We parked up at the hospital and I hobbled my way across the car park in my slippers in the rain. What a dozy mare! You'd think by my fourth child I may have known to phone the hospital and let them know in advance that we were on our way. I may have known that my husband could have dropped me right outside the maternity unit's doors. Somehow I managed to miss that so they weren't prepared for my arrival.

After being admitted I found that rocking side to side was easing my pain....that was until the nurse came in and told me I needed to be dripped up for a caesarean and I had to lie on the bed. This was a precaution as I'd had an emergency section with my younger son. I was gutted.

I was only in labour for about two hours. The nurse came in and told me at this stage if the baby wasn't going to make an appearance soon, then it would be down to theatre for me. With that I tried a little push and that was it, he was coming! I turned my head away from my husband and I groaned like a cow. I squeezed his hand with all my strength and hoped to God I hadn't ruined my image. Our gorgeous boy was born at 7 pm on the dot.

As soon as he arrived we were delighted when he did a big wee all over the nurse. At least his bladder was emptying. I breast fed him straight away after tucking his naked little body up my nighty and we bonded immediately. He had a scan and a blood test the next day and as his kidneys were still dilated he was transferred to Alder Hey children's hospital. I made the journey over in an ambulance with my baby tucked up in a pram beside me. I shivered with cold and wrapped my dressing gown around me tightly, pondering the future of my little one. My poor baby was like a pin cushion for the next two weeks. I was further away from home now and there was no way I was going to leave my baby and go back to the house, besides, I wanted to breastfeed him. For the first three nights I stayed in a tiny room in the corridor so I was at hand. I didn't sleep a wink. The rest of the time I stayed in Ronald Macdonald house. It was quickly confirmed that he did have posterior urethral valves and my tiny baby would now need an operation.

At five days old our wee man had to have an operation called an endoscopic incision of the valves. This procedure was to trim down the excess flaps of skin, or 'valves' that were causing the blockage. He had to have a catheter fitted until his fluid ran clear and he healed. At present his fluid was bright yellow and was thick with what resembled floating ripped up tissue paper, clearly all the toxins that were not being allowed to pass out naturally. We sat in the waiting room until he was ready to go down to theatre. I felt so useless as he was wheeled away on his hospital bed. He was like a dot on the landscape, a tiny bundle with wires everywhere on this hulking great bed. All we could do now was wait for news of how the operation went and we cried together. My arms were empty and our tiny baby's life was in someone else's hands. I remember his little face, weary with the anaesthetic when he came back up to the ward. So tiny but so strong! Sadly one of his kidneys didn't recover from the damage and he was left with just the right one which functions normally. His working kidney also has a baggy valve and keeping any infections away would be detrimental to his health from now on. Little did we know at this point the hell we would go through to implement this. Doctors thankfully said it would be possible for him to live a normal life. He was prescribed regular medication and he had to have check ups and scans every couple of months.

Having the chickpea has been one of the best things I have ever done in my life. He has been the most fun and the most happiness ever. He is such a blessing to us. That doesn't mean that things are easy, far from it. In fact out of all of my children, I think with him I have faced the most challenges. Never a dull moment though. From the minute he was born our lives have completely changed.

We are in a different season now. I went from retrieving some independence back in my life now that my other children had grown up a bit and they were a lot older, to a nursing Mummy again. I breastfed for seven and a half months determined to give the chickpea the best start in life. I went to *Booby clinic* as I called it and *Bounce and Rhyme* at the library and any other activities I could access involving toddlers and Mummies. He attended my nephew's first birthday party when he was just one month old. It was so lovely to be around my family again. Now my sister and I both had little boys of a similar age who I believed would grow up together and we could be close. The boys could be close, as cousins should be in an ideal world. My whole world was full of new opportunities, new doors to open and new people to meet. I met new friends with little ones like me. I even sold my beloved modified motor as it was now impractical with a huge pram to try and cram in it. No need for a booming sound system either now. However, I did hang on to one of my twelve inch subs (massive speaker). The pram would have to go on my back seat. Still a bass junkie at heart, my music was a must.

The chickpea was a very quiet and placid baby. He was beautiful with tri colour eyes; they were mainly hazel but in the light reflected green and sometimes a tiny bit of blue. His mop of light brown hair stuck up in a fluffy tuft at the front and made way for a large birthmark on top of his head. This birthmark is made up of broken capillaries and he had a smaller, similar one on his cheek. He was happy in his own company. He hardly ever cried and he seemed to be constantly contented despite all the trips up and down to the hospital. He was poked and prodded and scanned but he never complained. He would never go to other people or sit on anyone else's knee and even at toddler groups he would stick to my leg as if I had a magnet up my rear end. He would play by my feet but he never ventured from me, my little shadow. He loved the zoo and the farm and anything that involved water. In fact he is still fascinated by water and he will stand for hours just watching the trickling of a stream or a water fountain. One of his favourite places is the Blue Planet aquarium and in fact any other aquarium. He loves to watch the fish. He is what we have always called 'A Watcher' taking everything in and never missing a trick. He always stands on the outside looking in and watches everything going on around him. He loves sparkly lights and classical music and we found that this was great for soothing him.

Life has been a whirlwind of adventure with our little star. We did the day trips and the holidays, the toddler walks and the funhouses, the farms and the beaches. We have done the birthday parties and visited Santa, and all the kind of normal stuff that families do. It was a full house and with three grown up children and a toddler, and Christmases were utter chaos.

Pre- School

The chickpea started pre-school on the 10th of September 2008. I remember being well chuffed that I had got him a place in this particular preschool. It had a good reputation and it was two minutes away from our house. The school also had a Christian ethos which was most important to me. The pre-school and the school are two different organisations but thinking ahead I wanted him to start off where he could go on naturally to the next stages in the same place.

Obviously I was worried sick about him going on his first day. He had never left my side since he was born and here he was, not even quite three yet. It was a big day for him, all be it just an afternoon. I took him in but he refused to leave my side. The teacher came and took him by the hand and led him in to the class. I darted out the door before he could protest. The teacher did give me a call to let me know he had stopped crying and he was settling in. Phew!

I remember being extremely worried about him using the toilets back then. Given his medical conditions it would be very important for him to not hold urine in as this could cause a urinary tract infection. This in turn could lead to a kidney infection as he has reflux meaning the infected urine would be flushing back up into his one remaining kidney. He was only in pre-school for two and a half hours at this stage though so it was not too much of an issue. He was also still on infection preventative medicine so hopefully keeping nasty bugs at bay. The chickpea seemed to be doing really well regarding his condition. He had managed to avoid any infections so far and his six monthly blood tests came back showing his kidney function was good despite it still being swollen and larger than average. His good kidney was working for the two.

After two years of half days at pre-school, on the 2nd of September 2010 the chickpea started full time school. He was very subdued going to school for a full day. He was a bit of a cling on and a very placid child so I wasn't sure how he would cope with a full day. Over the course of the last two years the chickpea had been very choosey over whom his friends were. He would mostly just stand on the peripheral and observe what was going on around him. He always steered away from the boisterous crowd and had two little friends who were quieter than the average children in his class. I had a little cry outside the school gates when I left him but I think most of us Mums do this. We are seeing our babies off into the big world and it's as scary for us as it is for them. As a Mum we want to protect our children and make sure they are OK.

Big School

The school term had only just started but I had booked a break to Anglesey in the second week of September. When we came back from our short break it was the chickpea's fifth birthday. We opted for a Doctor Who party at the Space Port in Seacombe. One very cute little boy wanted to *be* Doctor Who! He loved to dress up and often we noticed he came out of his shell a little when he wore a mask or a dressing up costume. I bought him some new pants and a jacket, a checked shirt and a fabulous burgundy coloured dickie bow so he could be Matt Smith's doctor, the eleventh doctor. He completed his look with the doctors sonic screw driver and I gelled his hair quiffing it over to one side. I remember him having a bit of a hissy fit as his hair wasn't right. He was very frustrated trying to tell me how it needed to be. It had to be absolutely perfect or it just wasn't right. Such a perfectionist!

At his party we had a tour guide who took him and his small party of friends around the exhibition. He especially loved the wormhole which was a tunnel full of flashing lights and he also liked the simulated back hole. They went around the Wallace and Grommet exhibition and had photos taken by Wallace's rocket. The chickpea wouldn't stand with the others by himself for a photo. I had to stand with him and hold his hand. He was painfully shy. Later on he went into his party room. I had requested plain ham sandwiches and plain cheese ones. The chickpea liked very plain food and nothing mixed or any different flavours mixed together. Anything that was not separate or if he couldn't tell what a food was caused him great anxiety. There were bags of crisps each, Jaffa cakes and Maltesers on a separate tray to the sandwiches. Perfect! Who needs posh, fancy party food? Half the time it doesn't get eaten anyway. The amount of times in the past I have had to launch fairy cakes with just the icing eaten off

the top or the crusts from the sandwiches. Either that or us Mums
end up eating it so it doesn't get wasted and then moan about our
expanding waist lines.

The space port guide then put a Doctor Who episode on the TV
screen on the party room wall. It was the perfect party for a quiet
little Doctor Who lover.

On the 8th of December 2010 the chickpea came home from
school in a right old mess. A mess he had been sat in for several
hours judging by the state of his clothes and his skin in the nether
regions. He'd had an accident which had gone unnoticed for a
lengthy period of time. This was not the first time this had
happened at his school. Since him starting there in the September
three months prior to this, there were barely a few days that went
by without an accident of this nature occurring. It was very
frustrating for me and for him. We had been told previously to
when he started at the school that the teachers were not allowed
to help the children in that area. The chickpea would be expected
to take care of himself. With regards to this we had sat down with
him and explained that he would have to start being a big boy
now. The teachers were not allowed to help him with the toilet so
he would need to be grown up. Of course he had been shown
what to do. He was potty trained at just two years old but he had
always chosen not to be responsible for clean up duty and that
was fine with me until he was ready. He was only little. If we ever
left him in the loo encouraging him to clean himself up, he would
shout and scream uncontrollably for either me or Daddy to assist
him in that area, and he would scream until we gave in. It was as if
he had a fear of getting in a mess and he was just emotionally not
able to do it for himself. By leaving him to scream surely this
would be doing him more harm than good? He was more than
physically able but if your child is screaming to an extent where it
sounds like he is being murdered then what do you do? The
problem was, at school he seemed to just shut down where this
was concerned. He never asked for help and no-one was aware

that he required support with personal hygiene. I think that in his head he knew no-one would help him so he tried to hold it in. I hoped and prayed that all of a sudden he would just click. After all he was still only five!

Over the next few months I noticed how the chickpea growled a lot at people rather than communicating. I thought it was quite funny to be honest. It was just a funny little quirk from my funny little man. In school though, there was still no communication regarding his toileting. He still wasn't asking anyone to go and the teachers kept insisting they didn't know. I wondered why they didn't make a note of checking on this regularly given that it had been brought to their attention. Eventually I realised he may have been worried about going in to a toilet where other children were. I just couldn't figure it out. Did he have a fear of someone looking over at him or walking in on him? Did he not like the toilets? Was it because sometimes they were in a mess? You know yourself if you walk into a loo that's been splattered by the previous occupant you would walk straight back out! Something was definitely putting him off anyway. After discussion with the school he was allocated the disabled toilet which was on its own. I hoped to try and alleviate the possibility that other children in the area could be the issue.

On the 7th April 2011 the chickpea came home once again in a dreadful mess. This date was significant to me due to how bad it actually was. Although this had been going on every other day every week for six months now, today was particularly bad. As soon as he came out of school I knew. I could smell it. He refused to speak to me all the way home and growled like an animal, and an angry animal at that. It was no wonder. He was so sore. I got home and bathed and relaxed him. I asked the chickpea when he had needed the loo.

He told me, "before lunch."

I was seething. In that case this meant my baby had been sat in this mess for over three hours! I was absolutely fuming! After six months of trying to fathom out what the issue was, I got a huge breakthrough when he also told me he didn't like the toilets at school. This was a huge revelation. Maybe it was only a small thing, but it was huge for him to communicate this to me. I had never complained in all this time. I know it sounds stupid but I didn't want to cause any trouble or rock the boat. The school was always so apologetic that I felt bad if I complained.

However after talking to a friend and telling her I felt bad for complaining she encouraged me to do so by saying to me, "Why do you feel bad? He's your little boy, they've known about it since September and its now April. You can't let it carry on hun, as you say it is dangerous for him to hold it in. Honestly, kick some ass hun."

She was dead right. I phoned the school to complain and I was asked if I wanted to speak to his teacher.

I remember saying, "no, because I will kick off."

I was so angry. If I had spoken to the teacher I would have shouted at her in Swahili and I did not want to lose it. I passed a message on that I was not happy and that this could not go on any longer. I made the decision there and then that I would take my son home for lunch every day from now on. That way I could ensure he wasn't going a full six hours without doing what every human alive needs to do. I could not take the risk of him contracting an infection under the circumstances. I also saw the paediatrician at this time and asked him to write to the school to inform them of the importance of the chickpea's health and to reiterate the circumstances. On the advice of my friend I was going to "kick ass!"

The Letters

Dear Mum,

I have decided to write to you. Whether I send this letter or not I don't know as yet but I feel at least if I write, in my mind I have done something that could maybe break the ice. I doubt it will but I will write anyway. I have tried waving the white flag over the years but our relationship never lasts too long before we are presented with yet another problem. I believe in moving on. Forget the past. It doesn't matter anymore. But somehow I don't think you can let go. With you the past always seems to rear its ugly head. My head was messed up for a long time because of my past and it took me a while to work things out, but you know… I made it. I'm here and I'm sane! I have always had so much love to give you but always felt it was never reciprocated. I know that would probably hurt you for me to say that and that's why I don't know if I will send this letter. I will always carry a fear of hurting you by saying how I feel. But I trust God. I know that one day our relationship will be healed. However, just because I know this, it doesn't mean it will be healed right away.

You haven't spoken to me for two and a half years now; since just after I had found Dad after twenty two years. I found one parent and lost another, but then I never really did have you did I?

Anyway I decided to write because I have been thinking about you. I have been thinking about you since Mothers day. I mean, I think about you at other times too but this Mothers day seems to stick out in my mind more. I'm not sure why but I just knew I wanted to do something to let you know I love you. I wanted to send a card like all the other daughters who have still got their Mum's but I felt I would be a hypocrite if I did. A lot of flowery nonsense if you ask me! I can't say all that piffle when we don't even speak to each other. I can't say stuff that I don't mean. So I texted you and said I was thinking of you and 'God bless you,' because that's what I felt in my heart to say. You didn't reply!

I know you are probably hurt because of my book. It was never my intention to hurt you Mum. I just told the truth. I told it how it was but with no malice or hate. I have no malice or hate in me. It was not written with intent to condemn anyone or point the finger. Yes, there was a lot of stuff in my book that you maybe didn't want to come out but what you have to understand is that stuff did my head in for a very long time and now I can use it for good. I don't carry any resentment and I just want to share with other people that they don't need to let their past ruin their future either. I believe my story was God given. I know that God has worked through me to give my story to help other people that are, or were in similar situations to me. Mum if you could only see how many positive results have come from my story. I wish you could be proud of me. It is for the good not the bad. I know that you will only see the things I have written about you, the things that you would have preferred hidden and not all the good things that have happened in my life. I wish you could see past the past!

I decided a long time ago that I was going to get on with my life and concentrate on the people in my life that wanted to be part of my life. I couldn't go on fretting anymore about a relationship that constantly falls apart or was non existent. And Mum so many good things have happened in the last year especially. I want to tell you all these good things but I doubt you would be really interested. You decided not to speak to me anymore and I will not chase the dream of a perfect Mother daughter bond anymore but a text every now and again would at least be something. I personally don't believe in not speaking to people. How do you solve anything by being an ignoramus? I'm not calling you an ignoramus by the way. I'm talking in general now. I'm not bitter or anything that you don't speak to me. I can see it's easier on both behalf's.

Anyway I hope you are well. I imagine you have been out in your garden given the lovely sunshine we have had the last few weeks. I have been out in mine trying to weed it with my bad back. I feel like I'm ready for the knackers' yard some days. I think the neighbours round the front probably think I may be a bit mad too as I'm forever swearing at the bind weed as if it can actually hear me and might go away at my command. The chickpea has turned into a keen little gardener too. He loves to plant seeds and water the flowers. We have peas, parsnips, carrots, lettuce, tomato, coriander and a sunflower growing. Very big fan of water features also. Burlydam Garden Centre is a day out to him. I tell you he will be a cheap date when he gets older.

He has just had his hospital appointment last week. His specialist is very pleased with him and he doesn't need to see him again for another two years now. His kidney is a very good size as it is working for two and his bladder is emptying completely. Even his non working very tiny kidney has apparently grown a few millimetres. They said it would never do anything so to me that is a miracle in itself. I have been praying for it to suddenly grow.

He is doing really well in full time school now. I just love his cute little pictures. Little stick people and I get yellow hair and a smiley face. He brought one home today with green grass and blue skies. A very happy picture so in my estimation he is a very happy boy. He is getting very good at reading and loves writing (a bit like his Mum). Funny old soul though and he is what I call a watcher. He is very choosy about his mates and steers away from the boisterous little monkeys. He likes to sit off and work everyone out. He is very clever. He knows about gravity and asks the most random questions. Oh and apparently he is now a vegetarian! At lunch time yesterday he asked me, "is this ham on my butty?"

I said, "Yes."

"Is ham made of pig?"

"Yes that's right."

He said, "I'm not eatin it then" and threw it on to his plate.

His favourite telly is Doctor Who, and he could talk the head of a pint. Dad absolutely loves him. That feels really weird saying that to you. You went off the scene when he came on it so I've never really mentioned Dad to you before in a relationship kind of capacity. Since I was reunited with him two and a half years ago I have seen him nearly every Thursday. Every Thursday up until the chickpea went to school full time last September. Now it's not as often. It's just a bit more difficult to get there in the week now because I am working and I am involved with different things all week. We just get on so well. I see a lot of me in him. He always asks about you and my sister. I always have to tell him, 'sorry I haven't heard anything.' He doesn't understand this rift anymore than I do!

Well that was my first effort at saying something to you; even if you don't get this I still said it. I have so much more I want to tell you but this would be one heck of a long letter if I do it all now. I mean, I can rattle more than Mothercare so got to stop somewhere. I will write again. I hope you had a lovely Mothers day and Easter too.

Lots of love and God bless,

XXX

To my Granddaughter.

Hello my little chicken,

I thought I would write to you my little chicken. I know you are very little just yet and can't even walk yet, let alone read, but anyway. I hope that one day Mummy or Daddy will let you have these letters so you know that I was thinking of you even though I didn't see you. Things are a little difficult at the minute and so it has not been possible for me to visit. I can't explain to you why I haven't seen you but I want you to know that I love you very much. I know I am missing out on some important milestones in your life and you are missing out on your Nanny too. I pray one day that things will be different.

When I last saw you, you had left a smelly surprise in your nappy for your Mum. You were looking very bonny, gurgling and happy. I'm not sure if you have any teeth yet but don't worry they will come when they are ready. You must be getting very big now, probably busting out of all your clothes and costing Mum and Dad an arm and a leg. You are worth it though. You are the spitting image of your Daddy and I have to say the image of me when I was your age too. Hopefully that's a good thing. I really wanted to be the best Nanny ever to you. I didn't have a Nanny when I grew up and I know I missed out. I wanted to give you what I didn't have. I know at this stage you probably don't miss not having me there anyway as we didn't get to know each other did we? Never mind we will make up for lost time one day.

I wonder if you are going to a Mum's and tot's group yet with Mummy. Or bounce and rhyme at the library. Has Daddy taken you to Chester Zoo yet? You will have so much fun watching the animals. I used to take your uncle along to all these things. You will make some lovely friends and so will your Mum. Mums always need support when we have you little ones in tow. Well I will write off here now. I just wanted you to know that I have been thinking about you.

Lots of love and very big kisses from,

Nanny. XXXXXXXXX

Dear Mum,

Hi Mum, hope you are well. Just thought I would write you a line.

*Michael is approaching his eighteenth birthday and I am
organising his Hawaiian themed party. He is very excited. It
would be lovely if you and my sister could come. It is a family
occasion. I know that's most likely not going to happen though.
You have always been a bit funny about attending parties and
functions. I know you suffered with agoraphobia too although in
this case it wouldn't be because of that, that you weren't coming. I
remember you not coming to my first engagement party when I was
seventeen because it was in a pub! I tried to explain that it was a
function room and all family members of any age are welcome but
you were having none of it. You demented me at the time but it's
funny now looking back. But this is Michael's eighteenth. I am so
proud of my boy. He is doing really well at college and has just
been for a weekend away to Bala with the church. He has got the
most gorgeous girlfriend who I love to bits. He has been with her
for nearly three years now. You have missed out on so much on your
grandchildren. Does it never bother you? You never really had a
relationship with any of them. The chickpea hasn't even had so
much as a Christmas or birthday card for over two years. I know
that this is partly because of the state of our relationship but even
so you could have written or made a bit more of an effort. I am in
your shoes now. Things are strained with my eldest son. He doesn't
speak to me. They are angry and they don't know how to deal with
it all. Kids! So I don't see my granddaughter and I don't really see
there is much I can do about it. I'm best off just backing off. They
have told me I can't see her anyway so the most I can do is write.*

People do daft stuff when they are cross. I can't let it get to me. Maybe that's what you did. I understand now. There comes a point where you have to let God take over; give our worries to him. Why do we find it so hard to do that? God is there watching over us at all times but we still manage to get frustrated and angry about things that are out of our control. We have to remember that God is above all things and every situation. I hear this every week at church. God wants to be part of our lives and for us to turn to him when we need him. Why would we not do that?

There is absolutely nothing standing in the way of you contacting the kids now though. In fact there hasn't been for a long time. Maybe you should write to them? You used to write to me a lot when I was in care but you don't do that anymore. I did find a lot of your letters disturbing to be honest. They really messed me up emotionally some of them. You may not have realised that at the time. I believe you thought you were doing the right thing back then. I can see now that at least you were trying. Learning from mistakes though, I would say to try and be positive and not negative. Look at the good things instead of dwelling on the crap things. I have written to my granddaughter tonight. I think that it is at least something. I can't send it. I don't know if it would be kept for her or just discarded and of course she is too little to understand what is going on. Not that she should know. It wouldn't be fair to her anyway.

Well I'm off to bed now. Got to get up for school in the morning and then go to work. Then it's the weekend. Yay! I have got a full on one.

Good night and God bless XXXX

7th of May 2011

Dear Mum,

I went to see Dad yesterday, as always, he was well chuffed to see me. His usually line is,

"Awww it's good to see ya."

Then he'll put a coffee on for us. It's hard to believe we didn't see each other for twenty two years. He still has that same twinkle in his eye I remember from when I was a fourteen year old rebel arriving totally unexpected at his flat door all those years ago. He is such a part of our lives now. Even Jim knocks if he sees my car outside when passing to and from work (He works just by Dad's flat) which is weird given that Dad doesn't see my sister but he sees the father of her children now and then. It is not Dad's choice not to see her. He did try. At Christmas two years back he did put some money in an envelope for me to pass on to her. This was clearly his way of trying to break the ice. I was so excited and drove straight to her house and left it with her. She refused to accept it and passed it back to me. I felt awful having to give it back to Dad. I mean…I suppose one could argue that he has had several years to try but I have had chance to hear Dad's side of the story. I know he did try in his own way. I know he did come looking for us and actually sat outside my house not having the courage to knock. Fear of rejection can be a terrible thing. I know all to well about that. He asked about you and my sister again. I feel dejected not being able to share any news of you both. I suggested he write to my sister. He was thinking of knocking on her door. I know my Dad and that would take a lot of courage for him to do. I am scared for him that if he does choose to call on her that she may decline to entertain him. I explained to him tactfully I believe her thinking is that she has done without him for so long that what would be the point now? We have totally different view points. I could of course be wrong. He knows it is too late to be a father but you can never have too many friends can you? The past is the past. I wish she would give him a chance.

XX

It was the 8th of May 2011 and I can't believe how miserable I was that morning when I got up. I awoke in floods of tears. Not like me at all. I had been up and down most of the night in pain which is nothing unusual. I had hurt my back six years ago whilst digging the garden when I was seven months pregnant. Stupid I know. We women are stubborn though. We like to get the job done yesterday. No waiting around for a man to do it. I knew I had damaged it at the time but I didn't realise how serious it was. Only when the chickpea was six months old and the pain was still nagging did I get referred for an X-Ray. That was when I discovered I had Osteo Arthritis. However this morning was exceptionally hurty and proved too much. I wasn't even sure whether I was going to go to *Life church* today which is definitely not like me. I loved my church. It is in the centre of Bebington and you can just feel the life it breathes into the community. It is not called *Life* just by chance. This church is not just somewhere you go on Sunday to sing a few songs and say a bit of a prayer with not much of a notion about what you're actually doing or saying. You feel Gods presence like electricity in the air. Things happen at this church and I was proud to be a part of it.

I came back to this church in June 2010. It was pretty much a light bulb moment. I hadn't been to church in a while and I felt a definite poke from God one day whilst walking down the road, to start going again. I had stayed away because I felt like a hypocrite in Gods house after some things that had happened in my life a few years back. I felt like a bit of a failure if I am honest. I talked myself into believing that just because I was a Christian it didn't mean I had to commit on a weekly basis. I had been kidding myself up until this point that I didn't need to go to church anymore. *How on earth do you grow with God if you don't get fed spiritually?* I would realise this very soon after my return. I had been in and out of Life church over the last few years, occasionally to speak to the pastor there. I had confided in her about some personal issues which I was worried about at the time.

She was a fantastic listener, non judgemental and really made me feel like I mattered. The rest of the church was also very welcoming. I soon settled in there making some genuine friends and wanted to start getting more involved. I became involved with managing the church's charity shop and helping to organize the weekly coffee mornings.

This morning as I say though, I was miserable, feeling sorry for myself. I decided though that this pain was not going to stop me from going. I had put up with my back for six years so why should this morning be any different? Why should I not want to go now when I needed it the most? Sometimes we let stuff get in the way. We let life get in the way. God wants all of us, not just a little bit. He wants us to bring our troubles to him and give them to him. Everyone has stuff they are dealing with. I went to church anyway and had the most fantastic morning. In fact the whole house was buzzing. Life Church really did kick spiritual butt!

Dear Mum,

I miss you dreadfully today. I had to fight to hold back the tears in church this morning. One of my very good friends quite unexpectedly came up to me and planted a meaningful kiss on my cheek. I turned to look at her wondering who it was and as I put my arm around her I became overwhelmed. I rested my head against her as she put her arms around me and I fought not to fall apart. Maybe she had sensed how I was feeling or God had spoke to her telling her I needed that chink of comfort from another Mother. It felt very motherly and I won't ever forget it.

I would just like to pick up the phone and have a conversation with you Mum or maybe go for a brew in town like normal Mums and daughters. I'm not sure why this feeling has not gone away since Mothers day. I have to be honest; I don't usually miss you as much as this. Maybe you're on my mind more because I have commenced writing to you or maybe it's because I am thinking about my relationship with my own daughter. I would love to spend more time with her. We passed our difficult stage a long time ago when we had a rough few years of not getting on. I found it very difficult to bond with my daughter when she was growing up. I didn't know how to be with her. I couldn't use our relationship as a template. I couldn't even bring myself to give my kids a cuddle. I suppose in my mind then, I was scared of giving anything of myself or showing any emotion for fear of more rejection, even from my own children. I worked out a long time ago that I had to break the chain. I had to break the cycle so I didn't mess my kids up the way

I was messed up. I have tried my best. We do meet up in town now and again, or occasionally I will be giving her a lift home from somewhere so I will stop at her flat for a cuppa. We don't spend enough time together though. She is always off with her friends or doing her own thing. I have to accept that she is all grown up now and has her own life. I am grateful that we are friends. That is something that could easily be taken for granted.

I could never tell you to your face how much I think of you or am missing you at the moment. I would be scared of the reaction. Do you ever think of me? Do you miss me at all? This is just the way it is now. We don't see each other or speak to each other. It's just easier. That way we can't hurt each other anymore. So if you don't want to hurt me then you must still love me?

This morning's message in church was about our dreams. Never stop dreaming, never stop seeing the stars. Our pastor also talked about seeing the bigger picture. I am still at the minute, not knowing where I'm going or where these letters are taking me. I can't see the bigger picture. Book sales are slow, (this would probably please you), although I do have another testimony booked in for June. My business is slow but expanding. I pray constantly for God to make my paths straight; to help me to make the right choices in life.

Well I have just had a lovely roast chicken dinner and my husband is waiting for me to finish up here so we can go out for a drive. It's been raining for two days so we haven't really been out anywhere. I'll write again when I have more stuff to tell you.

Bye for now.

X

Puddles

That had to be the funniest thing I've seen in a while...about forty parents huddled together like penguins in the onslaught of hail, thunder and lightening. Lots of screaming and people falling down...Hilarious!

It was the 7th June 2011. There was a thunder storm today. And I mean it belted it down. Not just rain but hail and lightening.....in June! Mad English weather! I was picking the chickpea up from school and we got caught in it. Parents waited underneath the school canopy in the hope it would go off. Most of us got a good leg lashing as the hail whipped down on us and we screamed in unison with utter hilarity. I hung on for a few minutes and then decided to make a run for it. As soon as I emerged from the canopy I was drenched to the skin. This hail storm was taking no prisoners. As I ran with the chickpea I could hear his excitement and I began to laugh with him. Kids just have no fear do they? My hair was a tangled mass and I couldn't see where I was going. The rain was just belting down with not a chance of stopping. We approached a road where we stopped at the kerb to let an ongoing car pass. There was a huge puddle directly in front of the kerb. Without hesitation I shouted to the chickpea, "JUMP!" We both jumped hand in hand to the amusement of the driver looking to her right and straight at us. We roared with laughter as the puddle splashed up around us. Well we couldn't possibly have been any wetter so why not? It was fun.

Later on that day I was thinking about this. I didn't know how big that puddle was. It could have been a lot deeper than I had bargained for. It was a murky puddle so you couldn't see the bottom of it either. I had thought 'hmmm,' life is a bit like puddles and the weather isn't it, sometimes a bit murky? Sometimes the puddles of life are so big we walk around them or jump over them. Sometimes in life things or circumstances can seem too big for us. Dealing with situations in life can be too inconvenient a bit like the puddles and the weather. But isn't that what life is all about? We like to avoid certain situations or confrontation. We want to avoid a soaking or stepping in something we can't see. We can't see the bottom or the outcome so we don't want to take the risk. Getting wet is far too inconvenient. But my innocent child with no fear dived straight in at my command. Shouldn't we all be a bit more like that? All he saw was the fun in it and getting wet was just fabulous in his eyes.

The chickpea and I had taken a risk and jumped into that huge puddle not knowing how deep it was. We got absolutely soaked but it was worth it. If you jump into life like an innocent child then it can be worth it. Face your fears, troubles and inconveniences head on. They may be worth the risk and they may not be what you had expected. Your troubles may not be as deep as you thought. You could spend all your life avoiding the puddles or the rain or the wind, but what fun would that be? However, the puddle I was in right now was going to get deeper and I would soon feel like I was drowning.

More Letters

Dear Mum,

It was my birthday yesterday. I know you know that because you gave birth to me, but I just wanted you to know I was thinking about you. I thought about you the Saturday before my birthday because usually if you send me a card, it will land on the mat a good few days before. You are always very particular about sending it early to make sure it arrives at its destination on time. I haven't had a birthday card for a few years now but I waited out for the post anyway…just in case. It didn't come on the Saturday before so then I kept an eye out on my actual birthday. I really didn't think you would send me a card, but anyway I still waited. I hoped that you would send me one. I went out that morning to my family group. They spoilt me rotten with a box of celebrations, a card and a lovely bottle of rose. I had a lovely morning with friends and we chatted about the previous Friday when we had been out to celebrate my birthday and incorporated it with a charity night being held in Liverpool. We all got some fantastic bargains and we had a vintage tea party. You would have loved it. There were little china teapots and tea cups. The tables were all laid out with flowery table clothes and there were cake stands on each table with the most gorgeous hand made cupcakes on. It was a lovely evening. Then we went out for cocktails afterwards.

Anyway after family group I came home to the post but there was nothing on the mat from you. No card, no message, nothing! Couldn't you just have texted me? I'm a big believer in not saying something you don't mean. I never buy cards with all that smushy stuff unless I mean it but surely you were thinking of me, just a little? Could you not even have just sent me a text saying, 'Thinking of you or Have a nice day? I guess not!

X

In June of 2011 came sports day at school. The chickpea refused to wear his P E kit which was nothing unusual. We had always thought he just wanted his privacy; which he did of course and that was fine. He hated joining in any of these things and I watched him standing there on his own looking isolated. He was the same with the nativity plays, always looking very awkward and uncomfortable on the stage with his back toward the on looking parents. He was avoiding eye contact. He was the same in school assemblies, never going up to the front to collect an award or to do a speaking part. I had often become very tearful watching him, willing him in my mind to be brave. Fists clenched praying, 'you can do it son!'

He did one running race that year and I was amazed he even did that. He just took his own pace, completely not grasping the concept of winning. He was totally in a world of his own, but the taking part made me proud.

At the end of June we needed a break. I took the chickpea out of school for a week and we went to Tenby in South Wales. It was much needed. There is something about all that fresh air and sea breeze that just makes us come alive. The chickpea seems to just become one with nature and is the most relaxed and happy ever. We never have any issues when we go away. He loves to stay in the caravans and when playing on the beach he can carry on for hours without a care in the world. We went to Tenby's dinosaur park where we played crazy golf which he likes probably because it doesn't involve anyone else. We also visited several castles including Carew Castle and Tidal mill, Pembroke Castle and Manorbier Castle. We all buzz from climbing round and round up the spiral towers and investigating these beautiful medieval buildings. He never complains and seems to love doing all this stuff rather than theme parks and running wild. In the evenings we went to the show bars but we didn't stay too long as the noise was too much for him. He absolutely loves the lights though.

Dear Mum,

I was on my way to my friend's house in the car today. I had one of my worship CD's on and I was making my own holy racket in the car and I became a bit overwhelmed. I have already told you that I have been thinking about you a lot lately and this weekend has been no exception.

Anyway I became a bit emotional and felt that God really spoke to me. I just felt an urge to tell you I love you and my eyes started to fill with tears. I felt that no matter what, it was important to show love. I seized my moment at the traffic lights. Just a few words but I felt that it was something that I should do. I texted you 'I love you Mum x.'
I drove on to my destination thinking, will you text me back. How will you react, will you even care? The day passed; nothing! Clearly you are still angry then. If one of my children sent me that message I couldn't ignore it. I would melt. We have spent enough time fighting and having a hard time. It's time to get over it. Just let your guard down for heavens sake Mum. Your heart must be as hard as nails. Can't you see all I ever wanted was your love and that I love you? I felt I didn't get it, so spent a life time looking elsewhere. I have just told my story how it was and that's it. Let's move on.

I love you Mum X

Dear Sister,

Wow! It's the middle of August and the rain is bashing it down. It was lovely earlier. The sun was shining. I have been out to my lovely friend's house today and we took the kids to the park for a play. But now it's pouring down. I've done well to keep the chickpea entertained during the summer holidays given this weather. We have had a film day with popcorn and we shut the curtains for authenticity. We have been to the World Museum in Liverpool and on the few rain-free days we have managed the parks and garden centres. Anything cheap and cheerful will do for me. It can be an expensive do if you're not careful. Last week I went to Cheshire Oaks for a spot of shopping. My thinking was it was undercover and there is also a play area undercover. A friend and I got to do a bit of shopping (which ended up being school shoes) and then topped it off with coffee and muffins while the kids played undercover, out of the rain. We had been walking round to the play area when I saw you. There you were dashing past with the pram and I assume the boys. I didn't have time to think. I had actually been thinking about you this week and had a feeling I was going to bump into you or hear from you but I wasn't prepared to see you here. Silly me.

I was strolling along looking in all the shop windows and chatting away. The chickpea was running along with my friends little one. Did you see him? I expect you wouldn't recognise him as it has been nearly three years now since we saw you last. I don't know if you saw me. You were on the other side of the pavement area and I only saw you passing by chance as I turned back away from my gaze through the shop windows. I was stumped. I just stared back at you as you walked away not knowing what to do. If you had seen me, you had not wanted to stop so I didn't want to shout you and then be ignored by you. That old rejection thing still creeps in. I so wondered about the little baby in the pram that I have never seen. If you had been directly in front of me I would have stopped you without a doubt. Maybe you really didn't see me. I mean two kids and a pram in tow. I know how that is. I'm sure the more kids we have the more brain cells get killed off! Focusing is a mere memory when you have more than one child.

Then you had gone and the tears welled up. My eyes began to pool. I hardened myself and thought, 'Get a grip.' But we are sisters. It shouldn't be like this.

I hope that one day we are reunited.

XX

Changing Seasons

In September 2011 I decided to wean the chickpea back in to school for lunch times instead of taking him home everyday which was becoming very draining on me. I was dropping him off at school in the morning then going to work, and coming back to school at five to twelve to take him home for lunch. I took him home for lunch and went back to school for one o clock. At five past one I went back out to work again, then I was picking him up at home time. I was running around like a headless chicken. Not to mention having to catch up with house work, shopping and chores in the afternoons and entertain a little one.

So an individual health care plan was drawn up in a meeting at the school. As the new term started it was very important to put steps in place to ensure what had happened in the previous term did not happen again. I would now come into school to help with the transition, taking him to the loo to get him used to going in school. The chickpea was appointed his own teaching assistant who he would hopefully bond with and she would eventually take him to the disabled loo next to the school office. It was quiet here and he would not be disturbed or feel anxious. We arranged that I would come in at twelve forty and hide round the corner and she would try and take him. If there was a problem I could pop out like magic and take over. It was explained at this time that the chickpea would have impaired sensation to the urinary tract due to the operation he'd had at five days old. He would need to be told to go to the loo rather than asked and also he would need to have regular times at the same time each day. I also told the assistant she would need to knock gently on the door so he knew she had not left him or put her hand inside the door so he could see it and know she was there. I had found that this is what we had to do in public places to alleviate his fear. In view of this it was also agreed at the meeting that I would attend all school trips to ensure he used the public toilets otherwise this would also present a problem. Generally we used the disabled toilets anyway because he refused to go in the public ones. I never ever thought for a second any of this was strange!

On the 16th of September 2011, I had a feeling my season was about to change. Life is like puddles but it is also like the seasons - ever changing. I had thought to myself 'it may not change right now, but it is best to be prepared for it anyway.' Seasons don't last. As the Buds in spring blossom and bloom into the wonderful flowers and trees and the sun's warmth increases, this is how I had been feeling. My older children had all left home (get the flags out,) my little one seemed to be doing so well academically at school and my business was going really well. I was happily married and my first book had been published nearly a year ago. I had also been baptised nearly a year ago to this date. Life was on an even keel and I felt good. So I must enjoy the spring while I am still in this season. But spring always turns into summer then autumn into winter. As a new season approaches it is best to be prepared. As winter comes you would stock up on your winter woollies and your thermal knickers, give the grass a last mow of the year. We start buying Christmas presents and ditch the salads and barbeques for stews and winter warming recipes. So too must we prepare emotionally for life's seasonal changes and I knew I had to do this.

It's funny actually; thinking of my baptism, I couldn't understand why I hadn't been baptised before in all these years. I became a Christian a long-long time ago and really I should have taken this step by now. It says in the bible 'believe and be baptised.' I also know that God requires us to do this straight away, as soon after making our decision to walk with him. Why hadn't I done so?

Just before I started going back to Life church in June 2010, I had been questioning this quite a lot. I had asked a local pastor from a different church, but I was very confused about it. He had explained that as I had been christened as a baby I really didn't need to be baptised but rather confirm my faith. It still bothered me though. Having me christened was my parents' decision, not mine. I needed to make my own choice to walk with God. I questioned a friend and then questioned the same pastor again on a later date. He then arranged for me to come to a meeting to discuss it thoroughly. The date fell on my birthday and also that same week I found a little card that I had been given when I was about fourteen years of age at the Billy Graham crusade. On the note, it read that I had confirmed my faith at the crusade. I felt that I had an answer and so I didn't attend the meeting and left things for the time being but I still had an inkling that I needed to be baptised and God was calling me now to do this now. I was restless.

I had been at Life church for just a few weeks at this time. I was chatting to my lovely new pastor in the church's local charity shop where I had been working.

Right out of the blue she asked me, "Have you been baptised?"

I just could not believe it. It could not have been anymore clearer if it had been a bolt of lightening or someone was clanging a massive bell down my lug hole. I was being called to take this step.

I replied, "Its funny you should say that."

I was baptised back in November 2010. I didn't think that it would make that much of a difference to me because I had been a Christian for so long. I didn't think I would feel any different. This was an outward declaration that I had chosen Jesus as my saviour. I had made my commitment years ago but this was like a seal. It suddenly dawned on me in the week leading up to it why it had taken me so long to get here. There was just a lot of stuff I'd had to do first. I wasn't ready. I have been on a journey, a long journey. Although I had chosen Jesus as my saviour I was not really walking with him. I was not growing with him and never really had been. And I really-really hate to admit this but I'm going to say it anyway, I was what they would call in Christian terms a 'backslider.' AARRGGHH! There you go I said it.

All those years ago I had been looking for love in all the wrong places. My quest for it had got me into so many messes. All along God had been patiently waiting for me. He poked and prodded me now and again so I knew he was there but I never fully understood. He had a plan for me. What I went through was never-ever going to be just for nothing. It was never going to be just a waste. God was going to use me and he had been biding his time.

My moment came and prior to being dunked I spoke a few words and a verse from the bible that meant something to me. I couldn't wait. I looked like a right meff with my hair scraped back and my dodgiest jogging bottoms and t-shirt on but there's no point looking like a glamour queen to go swimming is there? I was fully immersed and took in the entirety of the moment.

Afterwards I went off to get dried and it didn't really hit me immediately, but gradually I became overwhelmed. This was something I hadn't expected at all. I went back into the church and sat at the front; alone, needing the quiet. The seats were empty and there were only a few people about as the baptism had taken place in a different part of the building. I realised that this was really it. Everything had really been washed away, my past, my sins, my shame, everything. This was a new start for me and the old me has well and truly gone. I felt like I was being filled up and the old stuff was pouring out. Just like a cup being filled to overflowing. As the sparkling waters flow in, the rubbish stuff pours out over the side. I cried and let it all go. I have never been the same since.

Since then I have become stronger as a Christian. As I said though, seasons don't last. I had been blooming all that year so maybe it was time all my petals went mankey and fell off. That's life and being a Christian does not make everything perfect. It does not mean that all of a sudden your life is amazing and nothing will ever go wrong again. It does however mean that we have someone to lean on when our season changes for the worse. Things can't be all good all of the time but we can at least be prepared. It is my faith that has pulled me through so many situations and through the winters of my life. It would be my faith that would pull me through the season that was about to begin and the drowning puddle that I was sinking into. But with my faith, winter will turn back to spring once more.

On the 29th of September 2011, the midday assistant facebook messaged me to tell me some fantastic news. The chickpea had gone to the loo all by himself after lunch with no prompting. This was a huge achievement. We were both so proud of him. She asked me if I would carry on coming in to school and I replied that I would take each day as it comes.

She said to me, "there is never time or chance to say much at school and I know this isn't the correct way but I am happy for you to pass messages here, like what you want me to do."

I agreed "I don't mind at all on facebook. I am happy to carry on coming in at about twenty to one, which should be enough time for him to finish lunch and then hopefully he will do the same as today."

We closed our conversation at that. I really didn't mind that we discussed it through my private facebook message box. I was just so grateful that someone was helping us. I really appreciated what she was doing.

On October the 17th 2011 I came in at lunchtime to find the chickpea already soiled. It was not worth taking him to the school loo as he was in such a mess. We needed to go straight home. I couldn't believe this after all the effort we had been putting in. It was a huge step backwards and I cried with disappointment. I discovered there had been work men in the toilet that day and it had been made unavailable. It was unavailable right at the point when he had needed to go. The poor lad didn't realise he could go somewhere else. He wouldn't have thought to ask. He needed it before I had got there and yet again there was a complete failure of communication. Not one person thought that the fact the toilet he uses was out of action could have created a problem. I contacted his midday assistant and asked her about the situation. She assured me that it was a one off and I let it go. The next few weeks were relatively problem free.

In late February 2012 the midday assistant was moved from year one pupils to year fives. She was now no longer available to assist with my son's health care. Unfortunately, no one at school had informed me of this decision. No one told me that my son would now be left to it with no support when he needed it. After several days the assistant contacted me with a short and to the point message.

'Check who is taking the chickpea to the toilet'

I was shocked. I knew straight away that something was wrong. I telephoned the school immediately but being careful what I said, as the last thing I wanted to do was get the assistant in to trouble for contacting me outside of school. I was informed over the phone that he had been taken by another teacher on two occasions but he couldn't do anything. Well in my estimation there were five school days in a week so what the heck had happened on the other three days? This also meant he had not emptied is bladder for over six hours on each of the five days. In light of this, the midday assistant was then asked to resume with aiding him. Obviously the change of assistant had affected him and the few times he had been taken he had clammed up. He obviously needed the same person daily. He needed the same routine. This much was obvious.

On the 2nd March I had another conversation with the assistant.

She said to me, "hi, I take it you called school? I am taking care of your son again. Glad it got looked at."

I replied, "Hi love, so sorry I did mean to get back to you to thank you for letting me know. I'd had a funny feeling no one was taking him regularly because he had said for a few days he hadn't been, but his teacher told me he apparently went by himself on one of those days. I rang them when I got home and they said another teacher had taken him but he refused to go for her so he has obviously made that bond with you. So glad they asked if you could carry on taking him. I hope its not too much trouble for you. It is a big weight off my mind. They don't seem to understand. When I was carrying him his kidneys were both damaged because of the reflux. If his kidney swells up now he is in big trouble so he needs to empty his bladder regularly."

She then reported back to me, "I just had a feeling he wasn't being taken and just knew I had to tell you. It's no problem at all taking him, just hope I remember now with being up the other end of school. So long as he is ok that is what is important."

I replied, "Thanks so much. You're a star and really appreciated."

On the 29th March, a week before school broke up for Easter, I noticed the chickpea becoming quite lethargic and off his food. At the time I put it down to the end of term and him getting tired. He was also sick on several occasions. On the Thursday before school broke up, when I picked him up I could see through the class window his face was very red and hot and he was rubbing his eyes. He was crying and I wanted to reach through the glass and take a hold of him. My stomach knotted waiting for the teacher to open the door. Why was he crying? Why hadn't his teacher seen him? His teacher informed me that he had been quite tearful for the last half an hour and maybe he was coming down with something. He came out the door to me and burst in to tears and was in an absolute state.

At the gates he started screaming at me and lashing out, "I want to go home, I want to go home" repeatedly.

Another child from his class stopped me at the school gates and told me that the chickpea had been crying all day. I was horrified. His teacher had said the last half an hour, not all day! The chickpea tugged at my hand trying to run and pull me home as quick as he could. I found out he had actually been sat out at lunch time in the schools entrance hall on a bench because he felt ill. No one had phoned me to let me know he was feeling poorly. He virtually dragged me all the way home crying every step of the way. When he got home he ran straight in to the toilet and emptied everything out. He had a temperature, a sore head, and a tummy ache and he was ill. I was desperate to speak to the assistant again.

"Hi Hun, can you help me? Could you let me know if you took my son to the loo today? I picked him up from school and I could see through the window he was upset and tired looking. When he came out he burst into tears. He virtually dragged me home and ran straight to the toilet where he let everything go and he was in agony. He had soiled his pants also. He had a high temp so I thought it was a bug at first. He said he had a head ache and neck ache all day. On the way home one of his little friends had told me he had been crying all day. Then just now at home he said he was sat on a bench at lunch time waiting for someone. He had complained of feeling poorly and he said someone did ask if he was ok and said they would tell a teacher but he doesn't know which teacher it was that came. He weirdly enough is absolutely fine now and my worry is I think he has been hanging on all day for the loo. I'm really upset that he appears to have been left for most of the day upset and poorly but I want to get my facts straight first. I'm so upset I'm in tears over it. I had a meeting booked on the 31st of January which was cancelled and it has never been rescheduled. I just feel like they don't care. Sorry to burden you but I know I can trust you."

I gave him some medicine and he had a good nights sleep.

The next day he seemed fine so I knew then that it was probably down to his desperate need for the toilet which had made him so ill. The midday assistant said she had taken him the day before but now she could only get to him at eleven forty five instead of twelve thirty. This was far too early. These small changes to the routine obviously seemed insignificant to the school, but to me and my son they were so very important and once again no-one had thought to inform me. The chickpea needed to go to the loo after his lunch and not before which explained him hanging on all day until he got home. This was unacceptable.

Over that weekend at the Zoo he was sick again and he was off his food so I suspected a water infection. Looking back at the pattern of him being ill and when it started, it all tied in with the week that he hadn't used the toilet at school due to the builders being in. This must have been the start of him getting an infection; almost three weeks before.

On the 31st of March 2012, we went to Chester Zoo. It was part of my husband's birthday treat. He was the big Four Ohhhh (fourty) on the twentieth of March. We had already had a lovely night out to celebrate the weekend before with friends at a Chinese restaurant and then a few drinks out afterwards but we hadn't taken the chickpea with us. We had left him with a babysitter that night which was a new thing for us. I had met a young lady at the church who seemed to take a liking to the chickpea and him to her, so we thought we would try it out in the December just gone. We stayed local in case we needed to dash back home to him. It had gone well on that one occasion so we asked her to sit again for my husband's birthday night out. We had never really left him before the December, except for one occasion when he was three years old. This was a few years back when he was with family members for just one and a half hours. We had soon got the call that he was unsettled and could we fetch him. My husband had to go and pick him up as he was in such a state at being left. That was the end of his night out! The chickpea was so clingy and he liked his routine. He seemed to fret a great deal if he was ever away from us. He also didn't really take to new people and a regular baby sitter was something that had just never came about for us-until now.

I wanted to do something extra for us as a family to celebrate my husband's big day, as we'd had our night out with friends and the chickpea had not been included (for a change). Chester Zoo it was. I think it's important to include the little ones in family celebrations and occasions. The more happy memories you can make, the better. The chickpea was so excited. All he wanted to do was buy a snake from the shop (a fluffy one, not a real one) to go with the one he had bought there a few years ago. I made us a picnic and we set off early to meet Nanny and Granddad there.

At the Zoo he seemed to get sick again. I noticed he had been feeling like this on and off lately. One minute he was fine and then the next he felt ill again. We sat down to eat at lunch time and he had no appetite, then after a drink of juice he threw it all back up again. I had to shufty him over to the bushes to be sick so no one could see. I put it down to the excitement. He was so tired and he slumped over resting his head on the picnic bench. I was very worried about him and wondered if he indeed had another urinary tract infection.

After lunch we walked on to see the tropical birds and I bumped into my sister with her boys-my nephews. I eventually plucked up the courage to go and tell her I loved her and gave her a cuddle.

At home I wrote to her. Again, another letter I probably won't send!

Dear Sister,

It was so lovely to see you at the zoo with the boys. I don't think a day goes by when I don't think of how you are doing. I always wonder if I will bump into you somewhere. Quite often I will catch a glimpse of a tall slim lady with her blonde hair pulled back in a pony tail. You have your big long coat on and are pushing a little one in a pram. I will wonder if this is the little nephew I have never met. I'll glance over to catch your face. You turn... Its not you!

But this time, it was you walking my way.

I was standing outside the tropical house by the kiosk with my cappuccino in hand. We had stopped to get the chickpea an ice cream and me a much needed source of caffeine. You were strolling along with the pram right into the tropical house where we had just been. I turned very quickly away so you didn't see me for fear of that old rejection again. Fear that if you saw me you wouldn't want to know me or acknowledge me. I pondered for a moment and then I gathered myself together and asked my husband to hold my drink. I said I wouldn't be long and I was going to speak to you. I didn't give him a chance to reply and left him standing like a tea boy with a vacant look on his face. I'd had this chance once before. I wasn't going to ignore it a second time.

I rushed in with the chickpea in tow. Through the doors we had not long come out of and I scanned around the tropical house for you. Surely you wouldn't kick off or not want to see your nephew. I hoped not. There you were with your back to me craning over a load of giant over sized turtles but holding the pram with one hand stretched out behind you. This was my chance. I had butterflies in my tummy and crept up toward you. I then gently placed my hand over the top of yours. It was a few seconds before you turned around. I could see the surprise on your face when you did. I didn't give you a chance to react. I just looked and swiftly said,

"I know you don't want to speak to me but please give your nephew a cuddle and let me have a cuddle of mine." I figured the chickpea was a good trump card!

We exchanged comments on how big our boys were and how much they have grown. Then I saw the little one in the buggy. Oh my word how cute is he. He is a mini you when you were little. I immediately fell in love with him. I was also touched when you said to him, "Go to your Aunty for a cuddle." I couldn't wait to get him out of the pram. He didn't stay with me for long before he went off with his brothers. I didn't want to say too much or ask too many questions as I didn't want to make you feel uncomfortable. I meant it when I said I missed you and loved you. I do! I also meant it when I said I had not done anything maliciously or to deliberately hurt anyone. What I have done has been to help other people. I think you must have known I was talking about my book but I didn't want to mention it and spoil the moment we were having.

My lovely sister you have been through so much. You are unfortunately where I was all those years ago, bringing up three children on your own. I know how hard it must be for you. Never getting a break and being alone at the end of each day. Days of washing, ironing, and no money, etc. I wish you would let me be there for you but that rift is still there. You are still hurting and working stuff out and that's fine. I know that things won't be fixed over night. I suggested we take things slowly. Maybe meet for a coffee at a halfway point. I don't think you will contact me though. I left it open by mentioning I didn't have your number in the hope you would maybe give it to me. You didn't. I didn't want to push you for anything. You said you wished Mum and I could work things out and that I need to accept her as she is. Sister you hit the nail on the head. I accepted Mum as she is a long, long time ago. This has been part of my journey. I didn't tell you, but I have texted Mum several times and had no reply. I don't know whether she would have mentioned it to you. Or maybe she has changed her phone number? Anyhow I am glad that you have worked out that acceptance is key to moving on.

I hope for restoration in our family.

X

Rock bottom

On 2nd of April 2012, at the start of the holidays I ended up in accident and emergency with the chickpea. I had just been to the doctors as I was now distraught over the whole miscommunication situation and the chickpea still didn't seem right, even now after a course of antibiotics. I had tried to take a urine sample in for the doctor to test, but it just wasn't happening. He was so stressed and he refused to pee in the bottle. And then I was stressed thinking about how I was going to get him to pee in the bottle. And if he doesn't pee in the bottle, how the heck is a doctor going to detect an infection, when I can't get a sample for her to actually detect. He screamed and he moaned and he carried on. I tried to bribe him and I offered him treats but it got me nowhere. I eventually got a weenie bit of wee which I could see was not right and I'm no expert! He had already previously been prescribed five days of antibiotic which clearly had not got rid of the infection, and in my opinion it had slowly crept back.

On going back to the doctors, I couldn't take anymore. I was at rock bottom and I started to cry in her room pouring out to her how stressed I was over the whole thing. It had gone on for too long. I needed help regarding the school and asked her to please inform them once again how important this situation was. Blood was detected in his tiny sample of urine which indicated that the inside of his bladder was now severely irritated causing bleeding. It was of the doctor's opinion and mine that the cause of this infection was due to my son not emptying his bladder for long periods of time. The lack of communication from the school was now having a detrimental affect on my son's well being and I was extremely upset. This was the very thing I had tried so hard to avoid. I was so very distressed over what should have been our Easter break and my poor child who had been going through unnecessary discomfort over several weeks. I totally broke down in her office and told her everything that had been happening at the school for the past eighteen months. It was a relief to get it all out and I realised that I had been holding it all back for far too long.

Astonishingly she said this to me, "Do you think he may be autistic?"

I gaped at her, mouth open. I was here over a toilet issue! What was she on about?

"Nooo," I dragged out in an uncertain tone. "Err… what is it?"

As far as I knew the chickpea just had a public toilet issue and was a bit shy, nothing more. What was this doctor on about? I was baffled. We were referred up to the hospital there and then regarding the infection, and she faxed through to them her other concerns regarding possible autism.

At the hospital we were asked for another urine sample and the poor mite just couldn't do anything. It was such hard work explaining to him why we needed the wee and persuading him to part with it. It was like trying to get blood out of a stone. He was obviously feeling very uncomfortable by now. We stayed in the day ward and he played with the hospital toys but he was very lethargic. Another doctor came and spoke to me about the referral regarding autism and asked me how I felt about it. I told him I wasn't too concerned as I had only gone to the surgery about the toilet situation. That was my main concern right now. I hadn't connected the toilet issues with anything else. He assured me everything would be fine and from what I was saying, autism was not the case but to go along to the appointment anyway.

By the afternoon the chickpea hadn't urinated for over twenty one hours and he was due to be catheterised the next morning if he couldn't go. He had a machine put on his tummy which detected how much urine was in his bladder, it showed 250ml which was a substantial amount. I managed to get another very small sample from him which was then sent off to the lab and it confirmed a urinary tract infection. His bladder had become much enlarged and this now put his only one kidney under pressure. There was now even discussion of his left kidney being removed completely if the infections persisted. I was devastated.

We left the hospital with yet more antibiotic and we went to Macdonald's for our tea as it was now gone five o clock. We were starving. I prayed over the chickpea in the car for him to do a wee. Odd prayer you may think, but it does say in the good book, 'ask and it will be given.' After our Macdonald's tea, Daddy took him to the loo and thankfully his little flood gates opened. Prayers answered. I have never been so chuffed for a wee in all my life. This meant he would not have to go back the next morning and be catheterised.

I made the decision as of that week that he would come home for his lunch again but on a permanent basis this time so I could take care of him at lunch times myself. I was not prepared to take the risk of this happening again. I had totally lost my faith in the school where this was concerned.

Over the Easter holiday, despite the chickpea feeling rubbish for most of it, I noticed how the he was a much happier child with no aggressive behaviour which had obviously been due to how awful he had been feeling at school. His moods were notably improved when at home and he was a lot more settled.

So, autism, was there something in what the doctor had said? What was this autism? The doctor in accident and emergency had briefly mentioned the information that my doctor had faxed over to him. He had told me it was probably nothing and not to worry about it. An appointment for a paediatrician who was expert in this field would come through soon but that there could be a long wait of fifteen weeks. Almost three months.

And so my season had changed. Spring had turned to Autumn.

On the 16th of April 2012, I had no choice but to complain in writing to the chickpea's school. I had put it off for long enough through not wanting to complain and trying to be a good Christian. But being a Christian does not mean I shouldn't fight for what is right. This is my boy's health and I had to start fighting for him. I reiterated that the chickpea was under a health care plan at school. I explained yet again to them that as he has one kidney and he was born with posterior urethral valves, it was and still was, vital that he emptied his bladder regularly. I reminded the school again that this had become a huge issue for me and for my child, resulting in my taking the chickpea home at lunch times a year ago to date. I reminded them that I had picked him up from school over a six month period prior to that and almost on an every other day basis he had soiled himself; he had also been left for several hours in this state which was completely unacceptable. Why were they just not grasping how vital this was? I didn't understand it at all. I added now that the chickpea may also have autism. Although this was not diagnosed and it may not have even been the case it was going to be further looked into.

And so I thought, 'Put that in your pipe and smoke it.'

Autism Came Home

It's funny, but my husband and I had actually had a discussion several weeks before all this commotion had arisen. We had just been saying how quirky our son was. How he is a funny little guy and he is not like the other kids. His games were unusual and he played best on his own. The few friends he did have were the quieter ones who he had carefully selected. He didn't like the normal things that other kids did, like football and parties or anything that included loud noise or boisterousness. He preferred sitting in the book corner reading. The way he growled at strangers and how his routine was paramount to his happiness. He would be far happier standing in front of a water feature than going to a theme park. He had always been a cling on and very close to us. We could never leave him anywhere as he would stress too much, but if his Aunty came to the house he was happy for her to take him out. Leaving us was fine but not the other way around which was odd.

My exact words to my husband had been, "something is different but I can't put my finger on what it is. It isn't a problem. I love the fact that he is different. It is characters like him that will go far in life. I love him to bits, my quirky little man."

So now, weeks after this conversation we were told our quirky little guy may be autistic. My main concern at the time was his water infection so I didn't think too much on it. But now, I needed to look further in to this autism and see what was what. My husband firmly believed he wasn't autistic, but I decided to Google it in the meantime whilst we waited for the appointment to come through. I Googled it and I started reading up on the list of signs of autism and slowly but surely reality dawned on me.

As I read on I started to twig that all these signs had been there but somehow we had missed them, I had missed them. There was

the lack of eye contact, and the communication difficulties that we had put down to shyness and his quietness. There was his objection to clothes labels which irritated him and sock rage. If socks had a seam they posed a problem. If socks were not long enough they also posed a problem. The tears began to well up in my eyes the more I read on. The fowl tempers when he would blow up and other odd behaviours. I read on and on and then I remembered a day when the chickpea had done something wrong and he had been sent to his room as a consequence. I heard him shouting and banging up there so I went up to calm the situation. When I got to his room I was utterly gob smacked. This usually placid little six year old boy had turned every single drawer in his room upside down. Every single item of clothing was thrown down on the floor. Every single toy from his toy boxes was also strewn across the floor. The wardrobe contents had been flung out and the bedding down to the bottom sheet was torn off in the foulest of tempers. Anything in sight had just been raged upon and thrown. My boy was screaming uncontrollably, red faced with a total loss of control. At the time I had pondered on this behaviour wondering where it had all come from.
I had muttered to myself 'this isn't normal.'

There was a time when we had been walking to school one morning and the chickpea was so distraught (for reasons unknown at the time) that he had wrapped himself literally around a lamp post and hung to it for dear life. It took me all my strength to prize his fingers loose and pull him off it. His legs were straddled around the post like a monkey. He was unable to tell me what was wrong but it was plainly obvious he didn't want to go to school that day.

Another time I went around to a friend's house for a coffee. I had asked the chickpea to take his shoes off as we were guests in her house and he had refused. I just thought he was being awkward and insisted he do so as I wouldn't like someone's dirty, mucky shoes on my clean carpet. The ruckus that ensued was baffling. I removed his shoes for him and for the next hour and a half he screamed "I want to go home, I want to go home," repeatedly. There was no break from the screaming. I thought this behaviour was overly dramatic, very odd, and I just didn't get it.

Hair cuts along with nail cutting were another issue. He hated having his hair or nails cut. It was as if it physically hurt him and I would shrug it off thinking that a hair cut couldn't possibly hurt you….could it? One particular time at the hairdressers he refused to get in the chair. I did my best at persuading him, offering a lollypop if he complied. I eventually got him squirming in to the chair but he screamed the whole time.

The hairdresser was not happy and snapped at me, "I can't cut his hair if he won't keep still."

I was at a loss. I couldn't leave him with half a hair cut! When she had finished and my little boy got out of the chair he was baulking on a mouth full of hair. He had cried and screamed so much that his cascading wisps of hair had fell straight into his open mouth and were choking him. I immediately tried to wipe the hair out with the only thing I had to hand - a tissue. The hair dresser then ordered me to leave the shop as she did not want him to be sick on her shop floor. Needless to say I have not been back to that hairdresser again.

I recall being at church where someone was praying for my son and had his hand on the chickpea's head. Clearly he was uncomfortable; it looked as though the man was performing an exorcism. The chickpea writhed around on my knee, growling and moving his head from side to side a bit like Stevie Wonder. The man's touch really bothered him. It was funny but uncomfortably odd.

There were the loud noises when he would cover his ears up with his hands or the crowds of people which he hated and he would cling to me trembling. Whenever I took him to the funhouse over the road, he would cling to my leg for an hour and refuse to play on any of the equipment. By the time he was ready to play and feeling secure, it was time to leave.

So was this autism? Were they right? If so how had I missed it? Why had I not picked up on these signs? More importantly why had the school not picked up on these signs? Surely they see children like this every day and would have guessed before me? I was so happy with my quiet and placid little boy who never made a fuss. I was so happy that he had hardly ever cried and always played contently. I was made up with my quiet little boy that was easy to handle compared to the hard work and challenges of bringing up my first three children. So happy he wasn't swinging from the chandeliers like my A.D.H.D (attention deficit hyperactivity disorder) son had been fifteen years ago. And so, I had been blissfully unaware.

Autism just kept playing on my mind now. It invaded my mind constantly. I had to know if the chickpea had autism and I now watched him intently. I started piecing together the jigsaw, all the little odd behaviours and quirkiness and kept asking myself was there a chance he wasn't autistic and had they had got it wrong. I prayed and prayed for an appointment cancellation to come through to speed up the process. Waiting three months was going to be torture. The more I watched him the more the penny dropped.
I went from saying, 'Nooo…. but what is it?' to, 'Oh phooey, how do we deal with this now?' We needed to know for sure.

On the 13th of May I had kept the chickpea off school. He was showing signs of another water infection again.

He had complained of a sore throat and I had said to a friend that morning, "Sore throat again!"

He had complained of a sore throat weeks before when he had contracted the water infection in March, so I gathered that it must be associated. He'd had three lots of antibiotic since that infection though, so I didn't understand why it would have come back again. He appeared to be just how he was before; lying there, lethargic and he hadn't eaten all day. I was worried it was a water infection again, because if it was the doctor had mentioned about the hospital removing his non working kidney if it kept getting re-infected.....I was worried sick that this would be the case.

It turned out to be a viral throat infection but the doctor had said I was right to be concerned as it could have been related. An infection would go right through his system from the top to the bottom. A precautionary sample was sent off to the lab. I wasn't taking any chances.

The next day he was still really poorly and another doctor's appointment was necessary. The poor lamb had tonsillitis. I took him home and tucked him up on the couch, dosed him up and snuggled up near to him. Around lunch time the phone rang. Usually I would have been out picking the chickpea up from school at this point but as he was poorly I just so happened to be in. It was the clinic from just up the road phoning me to tell me they had a cancellation for an appointment with a paediatrician....in an hour's time! She asked me if I could make it. Make it? I couldn't believe my ears. I had prayed and prayed for a cancellation and here it was, offered to me with an hour to spare. The wait had gone from fifteen weeks to seven in the blink of an eye.

"Too right" I said.

I was an absolute bag of nerves. Was this it? Was I going to get an answer at last?

I arrived at the doctors, gave my name in and waited patiently in the reception area. The chickpea sat next to me taking in his unfamiliar surroundings. I was so nervous. My tummy bubbled with anticipation. I was called in after a short time and took a seat in front of a very nice lady paediatrician. I sat the chickpea on the chair next to me. The lady proceeded to tell me what was going to happen. I would be asked a lot of questions and we would take it from there. She went right back to the chickpea's birth and how he was when he was a baby. I told her how he had been a very quiet baby, never really crying much and being very contented. How he had never moved out of his cot, not even to stand up in the morning and shout me. He was always exactly where I had left him the night before contently waiting to be picked up the next morning. How he didn't walk until he was sixteen months old, preferring to bum shuffle and throw out one leg in front of the other as he scuffled along. Then I told her how he liked his food to be in separate dishes and he didn't like spicy food. He even considered fizzy pop to be spicy and refused to drink it. He would be quite happy to live on plain pasta and grated white cheese if we let him. Different foods could not be touching each other. If they were mixed this would cause him great anxiety because he couldn't tell one flavour from the other. I told her how he loved lights and was obsessed with water so much so that he had no fear of it. How he would play on his own happily and how he clung to me constantly. She asked me about him playing with other children and that was when I was stumped. I hadn't noticed it before, but now that she mentioned it he didn't actually interact with other children at all. He played along side, but not with. Then I remembered when I had taken him to baby bounce and rhyme every week how he used to become agitated. When he was very little he sat on my knee in the circle of mums with their baby's, but after a few months of going he appeared to hate it struggling against me to twist around, avoiding eye contact or trying to escape from my arms. He had never sang or clapped or joined in. I had mistakenly assumed this was a phase. But it was a phase that had never gone away. I told her of the toilet troubles that had gone on for so long and how he was now showing signs of struggling in the classroom. There were no major issues but he was very quiet and withdrawn. After about an hour of intense questioning the bombshell was dropped from a great height. BOOM!

"Yes he is definitely on the spectrum. I can't diagnose today as I need some more information from the school but he has autistic spectrum disorder."

My wait was over but I was shocked. There was no doubt from her. No 'oh we need to do more tests' or, 'we need to see you again.' It was just a flipping huge bombshell. The appointment had gone from fifteen weeks, to seven, to this appointment in an hour and WHAM! And so autism came home to stay.

Thankfully I had a holiday booked for Quay West at the end of May. It couldn't have come at a better time. We all needed a break and we welcomed the time to absorb our bombshell. Everything had happened so quickly so now it was time to slow down. I had read up and found out a lot more about autism in the last few weeks and I was a bit more clued up on it. I became more in tune with my son for doing this. I had previously done parent craft classes and this had aided me in difficult situations already. I believe this was why I hadn't really known there was anything a miss with my son. Because I had been using good strategies in the first place I had unknowingly defused any meltdowns bar that one when he had totalled his bedroom.

So it was Quay West here we come. I felt as if we had come to heaven. We were truly blessed with this holiday. The sun was cracking the flags and our caravan was up a mountain and over looking views of the sea. We had patio doors which led out on to a balcony with a ship's steering wheel attached to it which the chickpea thought was fabulous. He ran around in his undie's as free as a bird. I had my groceries shopping delivered to the caravan and the first thing we did was a barbeque in the sunshine.

The next day was another glorious day. I felt as if God had handpicked this holiday for us. He knew what we were going through. Even down to the little birds chirping on our balcony, a teapot in the cupboard and a clean caravan. It is the little things that count.

We did heaps of fun things in Quay West, absolutely relishing the peace and quiet. No school runs four times a day. It was bliss. The chickpea swam in the complex pool every morning. There was no stopping him in the water. We took a picnic to Cernarth Falls and enjoyed a woodland walk. The chickpea crouched down over the rippling stream with his Dad and just stood amazed at the silvery threads wisping away down stream to a new destination. We visited Killgerran Castle where a huge ape of a barking dog turned the chickpea into a quivering mess with his hands clasped over his ears. We quickly shifted him past. At the end of the day we sat and ate fish n chips (the biggest I ever saw in my life) at New Quay Harbour. We were on the look out for dolphins in the bay but we didn't see any although they were apparently spotted there regularly.

Mid week we visited a honey bee farm where the chickpea learned all about bees and how they make honey. He was fascinated absorbing all this scientific information. We went crabbing and took a trip to Cardigan Wildlife Centre. The day before we went home, we sat outside a pub on the river Teifi and had our tea. And on our last day we visited Devils Bridge on the way home. This was a spectacular four hundred foot waterfall which we walked all the way around. Then to top it all off we stopped off at King Arthur's Labyrinth where we went through the mine tunnels in a boat and through a waterfall. All in all a fantastic week that was full of watery fun, stress free and just what the doctor ordered. We had the most amazing jam packed time.

In June, my fourtieth birthday approached. As I was going to be the big four 'oh no,' I wanted to do something special. We opted to ask the sitter again to look after the chickpea for a third time and I organized a night out in Liverpool at a Greek restaurant. I was so excited at the prospect of a night out. My husband and I rarely get to go out together due to our previously non existing babysitter situation so it was going to be so lovely.

I remember being stressed that day preparing for the evening. But if I was stressed, how was our boy feeling? It must have been hard for the chickpea watching us getting ready and knowing we were going out and leaving him. It was out of the ordinary so it would have stressed him. I was right. His routine was disrupted because someone else was putting him to bed. We were dressed differently, we smelled differently. Where were we going? What time would we be back?
We were out for only one hour!

I had greeted twenty two guests at the restaurant and had just ordered my meal when my phone rang. I could not believe what I heard on the other end of the line. My child was screaming mercilessly in the background, and the sitter rambled down the line and I couldn't make head or tail of what she was saying to me. I took my phone and vacated to the ladies to talk to her calmly but it was no use, she was panicking and had lost all her reasoning. I would have no option but to leave my party and attend to my son. With twenty two people all sat around I was in the most awkward predicament, gutted to be leaving my party but my maternal instincts taking over. My boy needed me and I couldn't get to him immediately. My husband came to the rescue and said he would go and sort him out and come back when he was settled again. He left me with my guests and the surprise birthday cake he had just presented me with before the phone call. He never did come back. It took my husband nine minutes to drive home and our boy had had the mother of all meltdowns. He was palpitating and covered from head to toe in sweat and was hidden under his duvet. He was a state - and the cause? At tidy up time before bed, the sitter had put his Lego away and broken up some of his creations unwittingly knowing what the outcome would be. In her eyes she was tidying up – in his eyes she had destroyed his masterpieces. He had attacked her and she couldn't calm him down. Then to drown out his screaming she had turned the music up which had sent him over the edge. My husband sent me a text to assure me everything was OK now and told me to stay out and enjoy my night. I did stay out and still managed to have a good time despite being worried sick, but that was it. This was the last time I would ever have a sitter again. I was deflated. It was no ones fault, just one of those things. Our son just couldn't cope being left, he couldn't cope with the change. I knew he would be fine with Daddy. Daddy is his inner circle.

Circles

Shortly after we were told the chickpea was definitely on the autistic spectrum, I opted to go on a six week autistic awareness course held at the Rainbow Centre in town. In my opinion every parent and teacher should do this course regardless of whether your child has special needs or not. It would help if teachers and other parents were aware of how autism affects not just the child, but a whole family. And it would help an autistic child if their class mates knew that our kids are not just 'a naughty child.' They have social and communication problems and are not usually acting up for the fun of it. Any behaviour is usually the result of stress or change; it is the child trying to communicate something to you. One thing I have learned on this journey is about the lack of understanding that goes hand in hand with spectrum disorders. I can't tell you the amount of friends, and good friends at that, even best friends that I have lost during this time.

The friends that think they are helping when they say to you, "Oh well its only mild isn't it?" And this comment helps how? Autism is only mild until you place the autistic person under pressure or in a situation they are unable to cope with. A bomb is only non destructive until it goes off!

Or the friends that say, "Well he is fine at my house."

Yes it is all hunky dory when the autistic person is having a lovely time and there is no pressure or loud noises or people they don't know. It is great when there is structure and routine, but what happens when structure and routine are disrupted? What people don't usually see is the storm after the calm, to put it the other way around!

There are the friends that just don't get it when you say you are really sorry you can't make a certain event or party because you know your kid will have a meltdown. You know that your kid is going to sit in the corner snarling because they have no idea how to communicate with other children. Your child thinks if another child brushes past them by accident, that child is hitting them. You're on pins waiting for your child to attack anyone that touches them or gets in their way. They are not going to eat anything because they have those butterflies in their tummy out of fear of different surroundings and people they don't know or the food isn't right, it's not how Mummy makes it at home. There are germs in the air from all these people and your child doesn't want to breathe them in. The noise and the crowds are too much for them to bear. The sound is all mixed up and they can't tell what noise is coming from who or where and they are trying to process it all. Then there are the candles and your kid thinks the whole place is going to burn down and we are all going to die and you know that the Happy Birthday song is going to send them right over the edge! They would rather barricade themselves under a table than be at a party and 'let's go home right now!'

Then there are the nights out that you decline because you can't cope with your child's reaction to the change in their routine. You can't cope knowing even if you do go out, you're going to be coming home after an hour because your child is having a meltdown and the baby sitter is going to ring you any minute now. You keep checking your phone which has now become an object of pinging doom. Or even if you manage to stay out for a couple of hours you spend the whole time worrying that they are going to have the inevitable meltdown.

There are the friends that ask you, "Well why has it all of a sudden got worse?" And there you are, on the spot, trying to explain something that you don't fully understand yourself yet, feeling as though you have to justify yourself. You are made to feel as if you are making the whole thing up or exaggerating it in some way. You feel like you're under scrutiny and being judged. Eventually your friends stop asking you to go anywhere and assume you just don't want to. They avoid you because the conversation is too uncomfortable. They don't want to say the wrong thing and you don't want to appear dismissive. You're struggling for support but at this stage you still don't know exactly what it is you need. You have talked yourself to death and have no more talk left in you.

And so your circle of friends turns. You lose friends but you also gain friends. You discover a whole new world of people out there that are struggling as you are now, and you didn't know anything about it. The door is suddenly opened to special needs, a different world. You make new friends who understand and are on the same page as you. I was blessed at this time to have a friend who runs a group called 'Parents and carers of children with special needs' on facebook. I joined the group and found lots of support and wonderful new friends here and a coffee morning ran by her specifically for parents like me. A new season was beginning.

The autism course was one of the best decisions I made. Not only did it confirm to me that I had been doing the right thing with my son and I'd had some good strategies in place, but it also opened my eyes to what an autistic child goes through on a daily basis. I learned how autism is a social and communication disorder. How the world through their eyes is not perceived the same way we would perceive it; how the signals to the brain take longer to get there, creating sensory issues.

In my brain the signals would get to the brain like this (I hope)

-- Signals.

In the chickpea it is probably more like this, slightly delayed or broken up.

---- ----- ---- ---- ---- ---- ---- ---- Signals.

So if you think about the five senses they can all be either heightened or delayed. This is called hyper-sensitivity or hypo-sensitivity. Autistic people are not one or the other, it can fluctuate between hyper and hypo. So one minute you could have a child in excruciating pain with the tiniest of cuts or on another occasion a broken arm and they may not feel a thing. You have no idea what their next reaction is going to be.

With some children there is also no awareness of where about they are in space. This is what creates a problem with personal space. Often your child will be right up in your face trying desperately to show you something and you need to say,

"OO err step back son."

Or on the other hand if you're too close to them it could end up with you getting a punch in the gob because you're too close to them. You have invaded their space. I tried to remedy this with an invisible hula hoop. I showed the chickpea my hula hoop by stretching my arms out in front and finger tips to finger tips creating my circle.

I said to him, "This is my personal space. You don't come inside this."

Then I told him to do the same and showed him, "this is your space. I won't go inside your space."

Then there is the flapping and spinning in circles or spinning his arms round and round in circles. And the lying on the floor, bed or couch with his legs up the wall, the jumping and the bouncing. Being upside down or spinning is what is known as self regulation. The proprioception system is the ability to sense stimuli arising within the body regarding position, motion, and equilibrium and the vestibular system is all about balance and spatial awareness. Autism in children means that they struggle with both of these. They need to get the balance right in their bodies and all this flapping and spinning business is sorting it out for them. So with that in mind I bought a huge peanut ball for the chickpea to bounce or roll on and a trampoline for the garden. I also decided to create a sensory room for him, on a budget of course. I purchased ear defenders which are a God send and lots of mood lights and squeeze balls which help to calm anxiety. I also purchased some visual communication cards to help him with everyday things like toileting or asking for drinks.

I also realised how the chickpea views people. He doesn't understand the difference between a friend and someone you know just to say hello to. This is why people who have known him since he was born did not see any autistic traits in the earlier days. People he has known all his life do not pose a threat to him. He sees anyone he doesn't know as a stranger or a bad person.

We have fun and games when our front door goes unannounced. I have now learned to stand behind the chickpea when he runs to the door seething at the impending danger. I have learned to fold his arms and tuck him into me then open the door. If it is someone we know he immediately de-tenses. If it is a stranger we usually get a string of name calling such as, "bugger, unknown, intruder" and "poo head" before he dashes off to retrieve his light sabre and waves it profusely at them. I just explain to our guest that he is protecting himself and I will proceed to stroke our door step friend and tell him they are a nice person. Unless of course it is a stranger in which case teaching stranger danger is of paramount importance.

This is how the chickpea sees people:

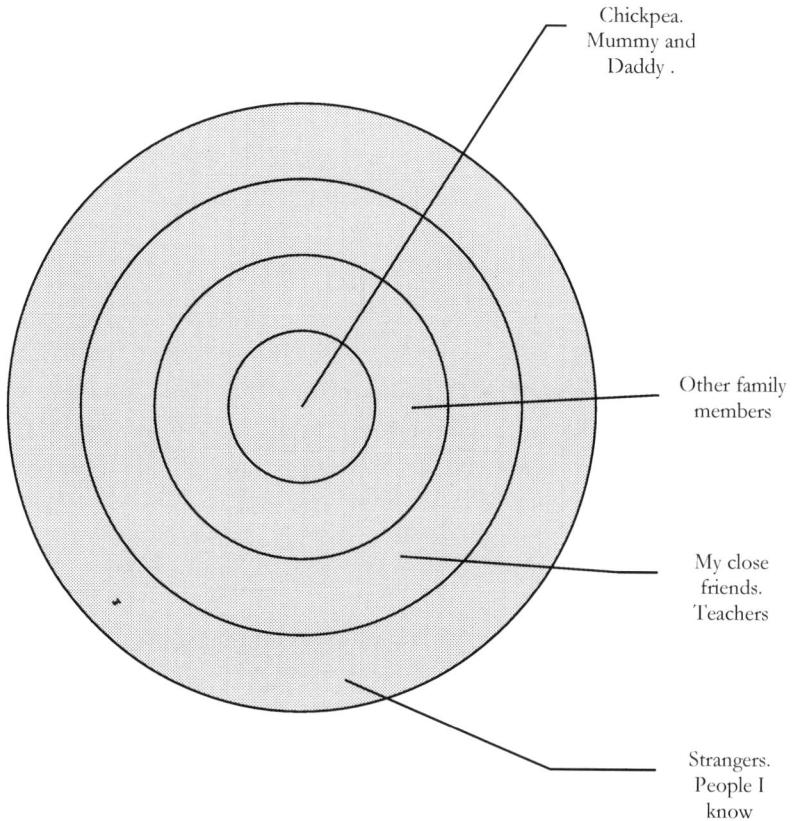

At the centre of the circle is the chickpea, Mummy and Daddy. No one else is getting in the centre anytime soon with the exception of one of his big brothers. This is his security.

The second ring represents other family members. His Nanny, Granddad, Aunty Carol, Aunty Sue and cousins. He often gets confused over who is a family member and needs a visual picture of where people fit in his life.

In the third ring are my close friends and teachers. My friends are OK at a distance. You may at least be acknowledged here. You are far from the centre and making him feel secure, but if you make an effort to get on my kid's wave length you could be lucky and move to the second ring. The chickpea's teachers are fabulous and are actually more like ring two. But if the teacher came to our house they would be out of context. They would not be where they are supposed to be and would be more like ring three. After a little settling they would possibly move to ring two.

Strangers or intruders as the chickpea calls them are most definitely in the farthest ring. Here you make my child feel insecure. He doesn't know you. Here you will be growled at and not spoken to. You have to work hard to move to ring three. You need to get on my kid's wave length but with no eye contact how will you do it? It has to be something really good. What are his interests? How can you make a connection? The worst thing that people can do is ignore him or decide not to speak to him for fear of upsetting him. You will remain a stranger and remain in ring four.

Wits End

7th July 2012.

To school 1,

I am writing once again regarding recent events.

This letter is further to the meeting which took place only two weeks ago with regards to my son's health care plan. As you know the plan was to take my son three times a day now to the toilet and also to introduce his year two teaching assistant so he may be able to bond with her now before September. It was also discussed about giving my son some coloured cards so he may place these on the table or give to a teacher if he needs someone to phone me to take him home to the toilet or if he needs to go to the toilet in school as he will not ask. I have also been told twice in the last two weeks that someone would chase up his doctors clinic to find out what information was needed in order to speed the diagnosis process up.

Firstly, I am not happy about some of the things that have been spoken over my child whilst he was present. At the beginning of July my son's teacher brought him out to me to go home for lunch. She complained to me that he had not been working that morning and she had had to sit with him for most of it. She complained that when giving instructions he was staring at the ceiling and was completely detached. While she may have had a viable issue, I found her telling me that my son had all the attention, so no one else in the class got any, and the rest of the class is suffering because of him, completely unacceptable. I feel that saying this in front of my child is not helpful and it makes me feel like my son is a burden to her. This is not the first time this has happened. I would also like to address the fact that if the teacher had to sit with him because of his behaviour, then where was the one to one I was told he would get in cases like this when he needs it?

Also my son on several occasions over the last two weeks has come home with soiled underwear again and has told me he had not been taken to the toilet despite the new plan to be taken three times a day.

I'm afraid I must also complain again at the state in which he came home to me last Wednesday on the forth of July. Once again he had soiled himself and had been left for quite a while in his own mess. I had to bath a very distressed child when he came home and his underwear was beyond salvage not to mention the stress this has caused me and my husband. My son told me he had not been taken to the toilet at break times and he had also been refused water because his beaker was not at school that day! He drank four beakers of water which measured the equivalent to three quarters of a pint and had a roaring temperature on arriving home. This is completely unacceptable and I am disgusted.

I do not understand how a health care plan is not being implemented after being revised and put in place only two weeks ago! Clearly the school cannot cope with my son's special needs therefore I will be keeping him at home until this is resolved.

I have spoken to his doctor's secretary who has told me that no one from school has phoned the clinic regarding the diagnosis of autism despite me being told the school would do so. She has also faxed over to you a questionnaire which needs filling in, in order to diagnose. I am not happy for my son to come back to school until I know that he will have one to one care and that steps are being taken to get him the help he needs and deserves. This has gone on for nearly two years now. Enough is enough!

I will never forget bringing him home on this particular day. I had never seen anything like it. I had absolutely hit the roof. An animal would not have been left in this state. I remember screaming and crying as I was so distraught listening to my poor little six year old crying, "Sorry Mummy, sorry Mummy," like it was his entire fault. From then on his confidence plummeted. It had been chipped away at for almost two years but this was the icing on the cake. The last few school weeks his behaviour had escalated and his anxieties were growing. Autism was becoming more and more apparent with the growing pressure of year one.

Despite the cards I had bought him to aid with communication, the chickpea had told me he was told to "put those silly cards away" by the teacher. She clearly didn't understand his need for the communication aids. The size of his class was large, the increased work, the loud noise and added feelings of humiliation which he of course would not be able to describe, but he was no doubt feeling, it was obviously becoming too much for him.

From now on when my son was distressed or anxious I would hear cries of, "kill me, kill me, squeeze me hard" or "I'm rubbish, I'm stupid."

He would hit himself and claw at his face. He would hide under tables or chairs and barricade himself in. I was heartbroken and as he was slowly being demoralised and his confidence destroyed so was mine. I felt like I was going mad and a depression descended on me that had stayed away for six years. I shut the curtains that afternoon and shut the world out with it. I was at wits end and hid myself away.

The letter of complaint I sent was a long time in coming. That same day, I discovered on phoning around various people involved, that although I had been told at the last meeting in June a statutory assessment was going to be applied for in order to meet the chickpea's needs, this had not been followed up either. A statutory assessment would take six months (two school terms) to complete and this would highlight the extra support being put in place for my son. They could then either apply for funding for a teaching assistant or they could apply for a statement of education. It hadn't even been started! I also asked the school for a copy of the letter which the kidney specialist had sent to them highlighting his medical needs. I was told this had been mislaid by the school. I complained to other agencies higher up as I felt that I was not being listened to. I had put it off and put it off for long enough but this was the last straw. So many mistakes were being made and a lack of communication was causing my son to suffer. It was time to put my foot down. I was sent a reply from the children and young peoples department with four different options I could take. It was all very confusing and with my brain full to capacity I couldn't comprehend any of it. Basically I was sign posted back to the school complaints procedure which had been getting me nowhere. I seemed to be at a dead end.

The school replied several days later and the whole thing seemed to be white washed over. It was just their word against mine about recent incidents. I was told that the chickpea did not want to make use at all of the coloured card system, but he told me he had never even seen any coloured cards! They tried to pass his soiling off as a tummy upset rather than their neglect. His tummy was upset because he had been holding on the whole day. The letter stated that I had said soiling was never an issue despite the numerous phone calls and emails regarding just that. What I had actually said was, it wasn't an issue at home but that it was an issue at school. Rather than them apologising and taking responsibility I was reprimanded for losing the plot with the secretary over the phone on the day in question after I had brought the chickpea home in that terrible state. I had bawled at her that my child was never going back to this school ever again! They had completely missed the point and failed to see why I had been so angry when I had phoned. There was no empathy at all. I think I was justified kicking off after two years of keeping my cool. After several unanswered emails and the need to text a member of staff out of school hours to confirm it, I agreed to a meeting the day before the chickpea broke up in July for the summer term to discuss his going back there in September. It seemed to me that they were avoiding having this meeting. I however, didn't want things hanging over my head over the summer holidays.

On the 24th of July, at the beginning of the holidays I received a letter from the paediatricain. Our little man was officially diagnosed with Autism Spectrum Disorder.

Rainbows

So, autistic spectrum disorder is a wide spectrum. A child can be anywhere on the spectrum. Where was my child on this spectrum? Did it matter? He was on it, end of. Even though I knew that he was likely to be diagnosed with autism it still hit me hard, and my husband too. He was no longer in denial. Unfortunately other family members still were in denial and this added to our stressful situation.

Like a rainbow this spectrum is a bow of many different colours, a bow that ranges from extreme ability or high functioning at one end to severe learning disability at the other end. Each one is unique, each child needing different support. In September my child would be pushed to his limits and I was still learning about his condition. We would now see how much support he really needed.

The chickpea started the new school term with a new teacher in a new classroom. A social and communication individual plan (SCIP) was established and a referral was made to Speech and Language. The SCIP outlined present behaviour that needed to change, specific targets for him to aim for and strategies to aid him in achieving the desirable outcome. Despite this, things deteriorated rapidly. On the 10th of September he was excluded from school for a full day. He had thrown chairs and pencil pots in the classroom, hurting some of the other children and the class teacher. He had to be held for his safety as he was putting himself and others at risk. The teacher had a bump on her head and scratches on her arm. I received a formal letter informing me of the exclusion and our rights and a load of jargon about not being seen in public during the exclusion. His behaviour was growing worse!

Then another incident on the 20th of September left me devastated. Clearly the chickpea could not cope in his new classroom with a new teacher. There were too many changes and his needs were not being met. He had been spitting and went into a huge meltdown and totally wrecked a corner of the classroom. He pulled all the books off the shelves and proceeded to fling them all on the floor. The classroom was evacuated whilst he ran amok destroying pupils work left on top of the tables. I arrived at lunch time to catch him mid flight. I dived over an upturned chair and sprung toward him and the mountain of books beside him. Clutching him up in a bear hug I held him until he calmed down. I felt useless. Why was this happening? What could I do? I needed a back up plan because clearly this school was letting him down.

A few days later I received a letter from school in the post. They were banning him from a school trip to the library as a punishment for his behaviour. I couldn't believe it. He had already been sent home for this particular incident on the day in question. They were punishing him twice for behaviour that he just couldn't help. I agree that there should be consequences for actions but I felt that this punishment was far too harsh. He had been looking forward to the trip and as I was listed on his health care plan to go on all school trips, he would not have posed any risk whilst I was present. I would have been with him the whole time. Of course, his posing a risk was the school's reason for the exclusion. I challenged his class teacher and the special education needs teacher who both said that the decision had not been theirs and they looked very uncomfortable discussing it. As I was talking to them at home time about it, the chickpea was in the corner of the room barricading him self in and placing chairs strategically around himself. He was making a safe haven. They were at a loss to know why he was doing this and the looks on their faces were ones of astonishment. Quite simply he was having a sensory overload.

I remember saying to one teacher directly, "He is not being naughty you know," as she humphed at him.

I thought, 'surely it would have made more sense to use this trip as a reward and use something else as a consequence.' 'Praise not punishment' as I have found out is a much better way of dealing with unwanted behaviour. The letter had also stated that further trips were at risk. It was clear to me that my son was not perfect enough for this school.

He was too much of a risk and they didn't want there image ruined.

I decided to put my back up plan in motion and made an appointment to go and look at another school in the area that had a good reputation for there intake of children with autism. This school also had a separate unit for children with special needs which could be accessed when the chickpea was eight years old. Although he would not be able to use it now, at least if he was already at the school it was to hand for when he did turn eight. It made sense.

That afternoon when we got home from school the chickpea had wet himself out of pure stress. He couldn't sleep that night due to worrying about going back to school the next day. I lay next to him on his bed in an effort to sooth him.

He constantly repeated to me, "The same thing will happen. The same thing will happen."

It broke my heart to hear him then say, "There is something wrong with me. I am trouble."

The tears trickled down my cheeks. I decided to take him to the doctor the next day and I had him signed of school for a few days with anxiety. No child should be saying things like this. I informed the school that his health would come before his education as it was far more important in my eyes.

Drop offs and pick ups at the school became very awkward for me. I withdrew from outside the class door and I withdrew from the parents banter. I stood at the end of the path that led to the classroom door and avoided eye contact with anyone. It was like being on the path of shame! I couldn't cope. If anyone spoke to me I just started to cry so I avoided the inevitable. I wondered if they were talking about me. I was acutely aware that some of their children had been disturbed by my son's actions and also injured. Most of the Mums were great and really understanding but the odd few just didn't get it. One Mum even told me how frightened her child had been of my son's outburst and maybe he should go somewhere else. I understood her and she was right but her lacking tact didn't do anything for my emotional state.

On the 1st of October I attended a multi agency meeting. I felt most uncomfortable. My child had just spent several days absent in accordance with the doctor's advice, and I had not been happy with the schools attitude. Now I had to sit face to face with the very people whom I had an objection to. The health care plan was reviewed and updated. The chickpea's paediatrician also attended this meeting and I was very pleased when she backed me up on my feelings about the school trip. She also did not agree with their decision and plainly said that any behaviour is a direct result of stress and if the school did not know what my son's triggers were, then it was up to them to figure it out. I was inwardly smiling at her support. I also stayed behind that afternoon after the meeting to fill in a CAF form. I had heard this mentioned a few times but didn't really know what it was. There seem to be a lot of abbreviations for things regarding special needs and parents are often at a loss to know what the heck anyone is talking about. Plain English please!

The CAF or 'common assessment framework' took around two hours to fill in. Basically this is an assessment of your child or young person covering everything from birth, health, learning, family, speech and listing all the agencies involved with you in order to get the support needed. I sat along side the head teacher who was very nice to me but I felt uncomfortable under the circumstances. Things had gone too far now but filling this form in with her was necessary. I felt that her sickly sweetness was an over compensation for how badly things had been going. It was very draining, wracking my brain and providing all this complex information but at least some kind of ball was rolling now, all be it a slow moving one.

That same day the chickpea spent time with his new teaching assistant out of the classroom and in a little room of his own. At last, at least he was getting the one to one he needed. During his absence the school had obviously decided they needed to put this in place now. He really seemed to bond with his new teaching assistant and she messaged me with his progress. She used lots of visual aids and sought outside help and advice. She was also able to discover what some of his triggers were and above all she actually communicated with me.

The next morning he sang going to school and on the way home he was really happy and he didn't shut up. He told me all about a chalk board and paper towels that had been the subject of some amusing antics, and he said that the room was really neat and tidy because his TA (teaching assistant) had done it all. He mentioned taking play dough in to school too but I said I would check first. He hadn't been this happy for weeks and it made a huge difference at home. Bless him; he must have just been so stressed with all of the events of late.

On the 4th of October the chickpea had a meltdown. He had tried to run out of the school building and had to be held to prevent this from happening. He fought with all his might and his legs had been going ten to the dozen in his attempted escape. He was very tired and anxious after kicking out. When I got to the school he was mid flight. As I would have been taking him home for lunch anyway at this point, I intervened and took a hold of him. As we got outside the school door and a few steps away he collapsed in a heap at my feet sobbing uncontrollably. His legs had gone dead and he physically couldn't stand up again. He clung to my leg desperately and I was devastated. What had caused this latest trigger? I thought things were going OK and here he was on the floor again. I tried to shift him to a nearby little wall so we could sit on it and I could calm him, but I couldn't lift him as he was like a dead weight, completely exhausted. I resigned myself to just get down on the floor at his level and hold him there. The sweat was pouring from him and he couldn't physically speak. All that came out was gobbledy gook. Hot tears welled up in my eyes as I rocked him back and forth on the cold pavement in an attempt to pacify. I felt totally inadequate. I am his Mother and I didn't even know how to soothe him. I was failing him. It took me around ten minutes before we could even move from the spot and we took a slow walk home. He cried for twenty solid minutes when we got back home. I lay with him in my arms until he was ready and able to tell me what had happened. He had been too hot, too tired and too hungry. All in all a total sensory overload. I took him to the beach that afternoon for some fresh air. It did him the world of good and calmed him right down.

His TA kept in constant contact with me over the week and she was fabulous. I was really pleased with how she was dealing with my son and I now had hope that things would progress. She mentioned to me the possibility of PDA (more abbreviations) and said this sometimes goes hand in hand with autism. She had took the time to read up on it and told me it sounded just like him and I agreed with her. Pathological demand avoidance is when a child will use any tactics to avoid doing something they are anxious about. She was positive she could work through this.

Ten days on and the teaching assistant had to take time off work. It was unfortunate but it couldn't be helped. School failed to inform me of the changes (despite this being on his health care plan) until I actually arrived at the school on the morning of her first day of absence. And this is when things came to the crunch.

When picking my son up from school on the 15th, 16th and 17th of October he was in a clearly distressed state. He was pacing up and down on the classroom floor on all fours, growling and trying to hide in the cardboard Victorian cooker that the class had made. The supply teacher thought this was completely normal and he was just playing. I was bewildered. What seven year old does anyone know who crawls up and down the classroom floor on all fours growling like a demented dog? He was practically frothing at the mouth.

After speaking to her on all three days she couldn't understand why he was so distressed. I explained to her that home time was an issue due to the disruption and could cause a sensory overload. I asked her to imagine thirty or so children all getting out of there seats, thirty chairs scraping on the floor. Imagine them all putting their coats on and the classroom doors closing and opening, thirty children chattering loudly and all bustling for the door to rush out to their parents. My son would be working out where the sound was coming from, who was making which sound and being visually stunned at the same time. It's enough to tip me over the edge never mind him. I also noticed that the tables had been turned round to a different position on one of those days and this would have contributed to a sensory overload and confusion. In his brain he would have been trying to process all this new information. Why were they in a different place? To him they were the wrong way round. Why had they been moved? I am no expert in autism but even I knew this. In fact I had no idea why he was even in the classroom at all as integration had not yet been discussed with me at this stage. He should have been in his tranquil little room avoiding such anxiety.

On the 17th of October my son was not offered any drinks in school. This was also on his health care plan. As a result he had a meltdown on the way home through being sheer thirsty. On arriving back home he drank three quarters of a pint of juice in one go. He had also watched a film in the school hall which was too loud and had contributed to distressing him. This was noted by me in his communication book for the supply TA's information so it wouldn't happen again.

On the 18th of October I picked my son up at home time from his little room to find him distressed once again and under the table throwing numicon (visual number aids).

I dived under the table with him, sprawled across the floor alongside him and said, "Are you OK son?"

He replied through gritted teeth, "I hate home time."

I told him, "I know mate. We can stay here until it's quiet, it's OK"

When the supply teacher entered the room I noticed the classroom door was slightly ajar so I took this opportunity to ask her if she knew he had a health care plan. I had a sneaking suspicion she didn't have all of the relevant information regarding my son's well being. It had been niggling me for days about my son's erratic behaviour since she had taken over. As lovely as she was, something wasn't quite right.

She checked behind her as if making sure no one was listening and to my horror she whispered, "Oh no, I didn't know."

I informed her that he should be offered regular drinks everyday and part of yesterday's behaviour had been due to him being thirsty and also the loud film he had watched in the afternoon would have stressed him out. She again said she did not know.

I then asked her if she knew he had A.S.D to which she replied, "No, no one has told me that."

Shocked; I rephrased my question just in the case she did not understand the abbreviation A.S.D and I asked her again if she knew my son was autistic.

She again said, "No," she had not been told this.

She told me all she knew was that he had to be taken to the toilet. She said she had asked him if he wanted to go to the toilet but he had said no. On his health care plan it clearly stated my son was to be told to go and not asked as he has lack of sensation and does not know when he needs to urinate. I was speechless, I wanted to scream.

At home that night it took me an hour to pacify the chickpea. He was on the floor in a state as he was so stressed. He lay there half naked, crying into the carpet and he wouldn't even let me touch him. All I could do was crouch down next to him and put the tips of my fingers to the tips of his so he knew I was there. The hunger to embrace my boy was overwhelming as maternal instinct kicked in, but I knew that my touch would only be benefiting me and not him. The burning sensation of welling tears consumed me once again and I held back to give him what he needed most…space.

He had been in the school hall watching the same loud film again. If only the communication book had been read from the previous day they would have known to avoid this. My son's meltdown resulted in my missing his parents evening that night as he was in an unfit state to go back out.

I was absolutely astounded that vital information had not been passed on. The supply teacher had been assisting the chickpea for a total of seven days. No wonder she had no clue why he was behaving in such a fashion. How can such important information have not been passed on and who was supposed to pass it on? I had given the school chance after chance after chance and I now came to the decision that he would no longer attend this primary school. I immediately sent a transfer form in to the local education authority. While I appreciated that efforts had been made, it just wasn't good enough. Unfortunately the lack of communication was the school's downfall. It was time to put my back up plan into motion.

On Friday the 19th of October I had to go in to the school at lunch time to collect the chickpea's coat and his communication cards for the end of term. I had asked for the communication cards to be sent home at weekends in the communication book but as the book was largely ignored my message was not seen. Fancy! Communicating in a communication book about communication cards and getting no communication! It was ironic really.

The special education needs teacher greeted me in the entrance. I told her I was not happy and relayed the above information to her. I told her that the supply teacher didn't even know our son was autistic to which she replied, "Oh.... I don't know."

This was the last straw for me. I got his coat and cards and I walked out with no intention of ever going back again. I was no longer prepared for my son's health to be at risk. I would teach him at home if I had to.

I complained to the school yet again and decided to take the matter further, only to receive a reply that just reiterated to me all the things that had been put in place. It was all very well repeating to me what should have happened. The fact remained that what was written down on paper had largely not been followed through and the communication from school was non existent. The head teacher was at a loss as to why she should have used the term 'A.S.D' to the supply teacher as she did not want to label my son.

Now here is a discussion that drives me crackers. People get so hung up on conditions being referred to as labels. If a child had a broken leg you would call it a broken leg. I myself have a condition called hyperthyroidism. That's exactly what it is. Without the name of my condition or 'label' how can it be treated? Who cares if it is a label anyway? Not me. And I am pretty sure the chickpea couldn't give a monkey's uncle. He knows he has autism. He knows he has extra needs. He is fine with it so why should anyone else have a problem with his so called label? This label allows him to access the support he needs.

For the next few weeks whilst waiting for the school transfer to go through I decided to home school my boy myself. This was the point where I realised I couldn't keep working full time anymore, so I went to part time. I had been juggling everything from work to home to meetings and numerous hospital appointments. I was heading for a burn out. I couldn't carry on running around like a headless chicken and then needing to drop everything to get to my son. He needed me on tap. Now the chickpea had to come first so home schooling it would be for now.

I went online and chose several different subjects to cover. There were lots of fabulous educational sites. One of the lessons I chose was about prisms.

We learned how a prism is a transparent object with more than two ends of the same length and flat sides. It is usually made of glass or plastic but rainbows can also occur through water droplets which act like prisms. The prism allows white light from the sun to pass through it creating a rainbow. This is known as refraction. When white light passes through a prism it bends and splits the light into its spectrum of seven colours. The spectrum colours are red, orange, yellow, green, blue, indigo and violet. I taught the chickpea the little rhyme to help him remember the colours and order of them. Richard of York goes battling in vain. The reason we get different colours in a rainbow is because the light bends at the different angles through the prism creating each different colour. When light passes through the other side of the prism this is known as reflection.

There are many stories relating to rainbows. We discussed these too. There is most famously the bible story in the book of Genesis where God sent a rainbow after flooding the earth. God was sad because the people had grown wicked. They ignored his requests to change. God regretted that he had made the people and he decided to destroy all life on earth to rid it of the evil it had become. But Noah was a good man and so God sent a message to him to build the ark. He gave exact measurements and instructions for this work to be carried out. Even down to the type of wood it was to be built with. God told him to take two of every kind of animal on to the ark (clean and unclean animals) along with his family and they would be saved from the impending flood. It rained for forty days and forty nights and the earth was flooded for one hundred and fifty days. Even the mountains were covered. When the flood receded God sent a rainbow. This was a sign of the covenant that God now made. He would never send a flood to wipe out all of life on earth. Whenever the clouds appear and you see a rainbow it is a reminder of Gods promise.

On a trip to Cardiff in early October I had seen a rainbow stretching across the sky as we travelled down the motor way. I was reminded of God's promise. For me it was a clear sign that God still had our backs. I knew that although we were in the eye of the storm right now that he was there with us. This storm was going to pass. God had a plan!

Genesis 9: 8-16

And God said, "This is the sign of the covenant I am making between me and you and every living creature with you, a covenant for all generations to come: I have set my rainbow in the clouds, and it will be the sign of the covenant between me and the earth. Whenever I bring clouds over the earth and the rainbow appears in the clouds, I will remember my covenant between me and you and all living creatures of every kind. Never again will the waters become a flood to destroy all life. Whenever the rainbow appears in the clouds, I will see it and remember the everlasting covenant between God and all living creatures of every kind on the earth."

A New School

Through November I kept going despite several more knocks while I was down. I tried to gather all the relevant documents from the school including the minutes from a meeting the previous July, and a copy of the chickpea's individual education plan. This proved to be stressful resulting in yet another letter to them to speed things up. I needed these documents to take forward my complaint and also for the chickpea's transition in to the new school. Then a letter arrived in the post to tell me that the statutory assessment for the chickpea's special educational needs had been declined. They had concluded that there was insufficient evidence of the school having sought, implemented and reviewed advice from the relevant external professionals. In other words, they simply hadn't done enough. I was gutted, but I shouldn't have been surprised. After six months of hoping the chickpea would get the statement, we would now have to start all over again. It was a huge blow. He had been accepted for a place in the school I had visited a few months earlier, and so I hoped, and was sure that things would improve here.

At the new school it was agreed to take the transition slowly. At first he would start with an hour and gradually the time would be increased. It was hoped that by January he would be doing full days.

On the 19th November he spent an hour at his new school with his new teaching assistant and he had a lovely time. He had a visual photo album of places and teachers at the school, a visual timetable with actual photos on the wall behind his desk and two other autistic children were at his table. This was a good start. The teachers went thoroughly over his toileting and I was happy. He officially started the new school on the 22nd November for just one hour and then from the following Monday he would do half days up until Christmas. He had an opportunity to be in the Christmas nativity play (if he wanted to join in) and he had a first school trip planned for the 12th December. I was so excited for him. I was confident he would now get the support he needed. This school had assured me they had worked with lots of autistic children before and they would have no problem with settling him in.

At the beginning of the New Year 2013, after having time over the holidays to reflect, I decided to take my complaint with the previous school further and to write to the school governor. Even though we had moved on and could put the whole sorry nightmare behind us, I felt it was important to be offered an apology and above all to be heard. Most parents would have given up their complaint at this stage and not take matters any further. The system is too complicated and drawn out; the parents are far too confused with it all and are stressed coping with their child to have the time writing letters and sifting through paper work to collate all the facts. The child's health and well being takes precedence and complaining goes on the back burner. Or in a case like mine the child has been removed from the school in question so parents would see no point in carrying on with the said complaint. I was tired and worn out mentally, and I really wanted to just give up. My son had left the school now so I didn't need this extra burden. Call me a dog with a bone; I just couldn't let it go.

Dear school governor,

I feel I must write to you to bring some matters to your attention! The last thing I have ever wanted to do is to complain but now in hindsight I realise I must do something or nothing will ever change for the better. After the catalogue of events that my child and family have endured over a two year period I feel that this is necessary.

I also wish for an acknowledgement that mistakes have been made and a guarantee that things will improve for other special needs children that pass through this school

Unfortunately after much consideration I felt I had no choice but to transfer my son to a new school due to the way his extra needs were not being met and as he was suffering as a result.

My complaint is this,

No 1: Over a two year period my child came home to me almost on a daily basis in soiled underwear that had gone unnoticed by staff. I had explained on numerous occasions that my son has posterior urethral valves and one kidney. It was vital he did not get an infection. He did get an infection which resulted in him suffering over a three week period. The infection was undoubtedly contracted as a result of holding urine in for long periods of time in the school setting. This would not have happened if his health care plan had been strictly adhered to. I feel that this was negligent.

No 2: From September of last year onwards things took a downward spiral. My son was diagnosed with autism which was brought to the school's attention immediately. Despite this, things never improved due to the lack of information and communication on the school's behalf to me or among teaching staff. His health care plan and home school communication book were largely ignored resulting in him being deprived of water and being exposed to very loud noise, thus causing meltdown situations.

My son was excluded from school in September for behaviour related to his autism. He was then excluded from a school trip in September due to behaviour that was directly related to his autism. It was also questionable whether he was allowed to go on any other school trip in the future. The health care plan clearly states that I will go on all school trips where possible, yet the head teacher stated she did not know this. This clearly shows the lack of communication as this information had been on my son's health care plan for thirteen months prior to being excluded from the trip. I had also assured school the day before the trip that my son would pose no risk while I was with him as I was fully responsible for him and he rarely has meltdowns when with me but he was still excluded. I was told by members of staff that this was not their decision and I gained the impression that they did not agree with the decision either but felt they could not say so. I feel that this is disability discrimination.

No 3: While things were being put into place and efforts were made, certain teaching staff felt that their hands were tied due to the head teacher's attitude and lack of knowledge about special needs. While I do not want to name drop as a few certain members of staff were just being helpful to me while I was at one of the lowest times in my life for many years, I do have two full private conversations which stretch over a number of dates from my face *book account. I have saved these documents but do not wish to use them. I would just like to point out that whilst I appreciated it, these members of staff should not have had to contact me this way at all. My son's welfare should have been discussed in the correct manner using the correct channels but they felt that they could only do it this way. I also had a telephone conversation from another member of staff who felt it necessary to telephone me on a weekend to discuss my child as it could not be done at school due to hands being tied and a disagreement of some of the head teacher's views. This is totally unacceptable and one of the reasons I chose to transfer my son to a new school. I did not want to be put in a position where I had to keep my mouth shut or people could get into trouble for contacting me out of school hours.*

Added to this I had to contact a staff member on a private mobile number to confirm a meeting which was not confirmed in the correct way. Had I not done so I would not have known whether the meeting was to go ahead at all the next day.

No 4: *Regarding the last week of my son's time at this school I must complain about the fact that the supply teaching assistant who was allocated to my son for a week was not informed that he was autistic. I find this absolutely astounding. This was the final straw before I transferred my son to his new school.*

The head teacher's opinion was that she did not want to label my son. This is completely unacceptable. This vital information needed to be passed on to the TA or how else would she know why he was on the floor crawling around like a dog or barricading himself in amongst the chairs due to stress. The TA was given a little information by his school class teacher who had previously told me she knew very little about autism. In my opinion this information should have been passed on by the SENCO or the head teacher and it wasn't.

No 5: *Lastly, a private confidential letter to school last year which was addressed to the head teacher was discussed outside of school by a member of teaching staff with another person. This is a breach of confidentiality and totally unacceptable. Again, I do not want to name drop but I feel that this must be addressed with all staff at this school.*

There is a communication barrier at this school and it prevents a good school from becoming a better one. I know I am not the only one to have had grievances where children with special needs are concerned so clearly it needs addressing. I speak for the many parents who are and have been too afraid to come forward and say anything as they feel that the governors will close ranks against them. I do not want to take this matter further; however if the outcome from this letter is not satisfactory then it will be pursued. I also have all the supporting letters, dates and documents to accompany the information in this letter and all the complaint letters to school relating to the above incidents.

So in short my complaints are,

: Negligence. Health care plan not being adhered to throughout.

: Disability discrimination. Exclusions which were punishment for behaviour directly related to autism.

: Contact between members of staff in the correct manner.

: Vital information not being passed on.

: Breach of confidentiality.

: Lack of communication.

I trust that these matters will be taken in hand and dealt with.
Thank you.

I did look up disability discrimination to put an appeal forward but discovered it had to be done within a certain time frame and that time frame had now lapsed.

I received my reply from the school in February, once again just reiterating back to me what had been put in place and all the efforts that had been made drawing up plans. But there was no acknowledgement that the said plans had not been adhered to. The letter quoted back to me dates that 'this' had been said, and dates that 'that' had been written, but there was no acknowledgement of the mess that my son had come home in time and time again. No apology! No acknowledgement that mistakes had been made. They failed to see that excluding my son from the school trip was seen as a punishment and could have been dealt with differently. They disbelieved my son had been deprived of water which made me mad. They then went on to tell me that they were clear they would not have conducted school business using social network internet sites and said my phoning a staff members private mobile number out of school hours was a sensible course of action! My complaint referring to lack of communication was dismissed by reminding me off a letter I had received regarding information. But no acknowledgement was made of the communications that had <u>not</u> taken place where necessary.

Lastly, no course of action would be taken with regards to my private letter being discussed out of school with another person. I had wanted to prevent the discusser from being in big trouble, even though they were in the wrong, so I did not provide the details; therefore it could only be treated as an anonymous complaint. I had only wanted the school to respond to this by talking to all members of staff, that way the culprit would know who they were but I could keep that one person out of bigger trouble. They told me they regretted I was unhappy with the care and education provided for my son but thanked me for my recognition that the school was a good one. They apologised if the provision provided did not always meet my expectations.

I still felt that I was being brushed off and the real issue here had not been addressed. It was as if the whole situation had been white washed over again. Put it this way, if things hadn't been so bad I would not have felt it necessary to transfer my son to another school. After two and a half years I would not take the risk of my son's health being in jeopardy any longer. I now had to travel twelve miles a day to and from a different school. I really did try to resolve the problems at that school but to no avail and taking the matter further was the only way I felt that it would be dealt with. I think that they probably thought I was going to just go away, but this was my child we were talking about and I would fight for recognition of what went wrong. I took my complaint to the Local Education authority and Offsted. More letters! The whole thing was exhausting. I was advised by both agencies to use the formal complaint route and take my complaints to the next stage which would be (apparently) stage four. I had not been informed I could do this in the reply from school. Funny that!

I had received a flow chart in one of the reply letters which explained the complaint procedure. I wished I had received it earlier, or maybe I had received it but my mind was so chocca that I could not comprehend it. The form listed the stages.

Stage one: complaining informally. A teacher, the office, a support or senior member of staff will try to resolve the complaint avoiding using the head teacher at that stage.

Not happy?

Stage two: The head teacher should acknowledge the complaint orally or written within three days including the school complaints procedure (which I couldn't make head or tail of.) Didn't they know my brain was fried by now? The head teacher investigates and reviews the findings producing a written response or meeting with the complainant.

Not happy?

Stage three: The head teacher investigates or reviews the outcome of stage two which includes a meeting within fifteen days. The local education authority may possibly be involved.

Not happy?

Stage four: The chair of governors establishes a complaints committee. The committee is made up of three governors from the school with the chair of governors present provided he or she was not previously involved. A hearing is held with all parties involved.

Not happy?

Refer to Secretary of State or Ombudsman for admissions.

So in April, I sent a formal request to invoke stage four of the complaints procedure as I pushed myself to take my complaint further.

Despite the new school's promises, four months passed by and my son didn't get beyond two hours a day. It was increased to a full morning in mid January but he couldn't cope and it was decreased again. He was becoming upset, trying to escape and hiding under the tables. Then on January 30th, the chickpea was very angry and stressed about his first full day. There was definitely going to be fireworks! At the school meeting to discuss this supposed first full day, it was decided that it was not a good idea after all. I met the educational psychologist on this day at the meeting. She told me she could not understand how she had never heard of my son or myself before now and even apologised for what we had been through. I felt as though I was finally getting somewhere.

In February the chickpea had a particularly rough day, in fact he had a rough month...lots of sensory issues including rubbing his wrists on the carpet causing friction burns and running around at school and hiding because he didn't want to be touched. I could only assume from this that someone was trying to get a grip of him? He had a meltdown at home so I got the foot spa out to try and soothe him. He carried on the screaming and shouting at us and he was still awake in to the late evenings. I gave him his liquid timer and prayed for a little lie in, in the morning. I was shattered.

The rest of the month consisted of him hitting himself, screaming, thinking someone was going to kill him and protesting that no one should like him and he didn't know why people wanted to be his friend. It was awful.

There was a change of teaching assistant mid February which would have been a contributing factor to his stress levels. The new guy seemed to be sent from heaven though and I was very pleased. He bonded with my son really well and things were looking up.

However, he didn't go on the school trip or join in the nativity play that were both previously mentioned. I found myself driving him to school for eight fifty in the morning, driving home and then leaving again at ten fourty am to pick him back up at eleven am. I literally had an hour and a half a day to myself. Going back to work was out of the question. I felt like I had a newborn baby at home all over again.

The chickpea did make some progress at the new school and some of his achievements included feeling safe and supported in school, good relationships with some of the staff, accepting positive comments and beginning to communicate his feelings appropriately. Also on the plus side we had started sign language lessons. The chickpea seemed to respond really well if I used a simple sign to him, and on occasions when he chose to be non verbal I found that he would sometimes communicate this way.

As he was only in school for such a short time, I was able to fit in a session every Thursday afternoon at Wallasey Library. This wasn't officially British Sign Language; however the signs we learned enabled my son to communicate to me when he was stressed. I had strangely enough had a three week bout of otitis externa the previous June rendering me completely deaf in my left ear. I remember how frustrated I was at how I couldn't hear properly in a conversation with more than one person, how I had to be looking directly at the person speaking to me. I also felt very isolated, even though in a crowd of people. It made me think about the deaf community and how much of a struggle it must be, and I was only temporarily deaf in one ear. So, this strengthened my desire to learn sign language, it was very useful indeed as communication with my son but also with the deaf. I felt God was using my son to open another door.

In April 2013 we had a very worrying time. We were up and ready for the school run but before I could even walk out of the front door the chickpea had soaked through two pairs of trousers. Obviously something wasn't right and he was complaining of pain and feeling ill. I knew I would have to get a urine sample from him and pop it to the Doctors surgery, not one of my favourite things in the world to do. I pleaded with him to part with some wee for me. It was always such a huge issue for him to wee in a bottle and he became very anxious, growling and hitting me. He managed a tiny amount after much bribery. It was orange and cloudy, clearly not right. I tried to get a doctors appointment immediately but there were none left for that day. The Doctor was going to phone me back at the end of surgery for a telephone consultation but by ten am the chickpea was urinating blood. I couldn't hang around waiting for a phone call; I needed to get him to the hospital immediately. Obviously due to him only having one kidney and posterior urethral valves, this was my worst fear so I was not taking any chances and I rushed him straight up to

Arrowe Park hospital. He was in excruciating pain when urinating and he just had no control over his bladder what so ever.

At the hospital they needed another sample. This time I had to bribe him with some Doctor Who collector's cards to get him to wee in yet another bottle to be tested. It was brown!

My brave soldier asked me, "Pray for me Mummy," whilst we were in the loo and we also prayed in the cubicle.

He said, "God is going to help me."

As the morning passed his pain grew worse and I felt useless. We sat in the waiting room and he screamed in agony through gritted teeth and as he stood up the blood splattered everywhere. He was bent over double and all I could do was stand there and rub his back in some effort to sooth him. I just wanted to take his pain away and endure it for him. All I could do was watch as he suffered and wait for the doctors to call us in.

All I could muster up to say to him was, "Its Ok. It's all going to be OK."

My heart was breaking once again. What was happening? Was this more than just an infection? I was worried sick.

After spending the day at hospital and watching him being poked and prodded he was prescribed with a strong antibiotic. The feeling was he needed a kidney and liver function test so I'd had an appointment with his specialist brought forward to May 14th. It was very important that he did not have reoccurring infections because his one remaining kidney is already scarred and any more damage to it could cause a lot of trouble for him. The doctor mentioned again the chance he may have to go back on preventative drugs or at worst have the damaged left kidney removed as it may have been that which was causing the infection.

The next morning the chickpea woke up with absolutely no pain and insisted God had helped him through the night and He listens to his prayers.

May 13th started with Family group which was very nice. I would rush there on a Monday morning and squeeze in my hour and a half. I was enjoying my toast and coffee, chatting away to the girls, and saying that things were going quite well under the circumstances as the chickpea had managed two hours a day in school last week and also the week before. I was made up with him. I spoke too soon. Forty minutes later my phone rang. Whenever my phone rang my stomach lurched. The dread of knowing it was the school again and this time as predicted- it was.

They asked me, "Could you come and get your son and take him home?"

I asked, "Why, what has happened?"

"I don't know, we think he is going to have a meltdown!"

Think? I was a bit miffed to be honest. Forty minutes! What was all that about? He only did two hours a day and they couldn't manage him for forty minutes?

I arrived at the school, and he was sitting there in the entrance hall as quiet as a mouse, no sign what so ever of a meltdown. The teaching assistant then went on to tell me that he was becoming agitated, had ripped a poster up and they couldn't have him running around in school today as there were exams in the hall. His quiet room was being used by someone else so they couldn't go in there. Well, I had to tell him I was annoyed as I didn't think this was a basis for sending him home. Provisions should have been made for him in light of the exams. Surely they should have made other arrangements if his room was being used? I said that the school needed to be detectives and work out why he was agitated in the first place and not phone me at the first hint of a problem. The chickpea told me straight away that he didn't understand fractions. He wanted to go back into class, he wanted to do the work but he didn't understand it. I told the teaching assistant there and then to take him back in to class, which he did and the chickpea then stayed for an extra ten minutes on top of his usual two hours. The moral of this story is *'Mother knows best.'*

I was so proud of him for going back in to school and proving my point that its not that he wants to go home, or that he kicks off to go home, It's that he actually needs the extra one to one and for someone to support him to stay in school and for someone to have an idea of what is going on in his head….which I do.

When I picked my boy up at eleven am he had not been taken to the toilet at ten thirty am as he should have been before break time. The teaching assistant said he had not wanted to disturb the chickpea as he was settled at the time. 'Here we go again' I thought. I could see that things were slipping and I didn't want to end up in a situation as I had been previously. I felt another letter coming on.

I went in to speak to the class teacher regarding this and then followed it up in writing charting my concerns. I yet again stressed the importance of my son going to the toilet. I had created a toilet chart for him and sent it in to school which he had responded well to the previous Friday earning a sticker. He also responded well a second time going to the toilet again but then he did not get a reward sticker? This may have confused him. Consistency was vital. This was a simple thing and he really needed to be encouraged in this area. I discussed this with the class teacher who said she had thought I was coming in to take him to the toilet before break time as that was the arrangement that was discussed at the last meeting. Unfortunately, I had asked on several occasions what time play time break would be so I could come in at the right time, but it was never verified so I'd had to guess. Anyhow I had felt it better that the teaching assistant at least attempted to get him to go without my presence in view of trying to encourage the chickpea to stay in school for a longer period of time. If the teaching assistant failed to get him to go, I could take him at eleven am when I picked him up, as a last resort. The point was, the teaching assistant hadn't even made the attempt before the break. Things were just getting confused. Things really shouldn't have been this complicated. It wasn't rocket science!

I also needed to ask the teacher why the incontinence nurse had not been contacted. This had been noted at the school review in March. I had bumped into the incontinence nurse by chance the following May (two months later) who informed me she knew nothing about it. No one had contacted her and she knew nothing about an upcoming meeting in June. I was starting to face the reality that even in this new school my son could not cope and needed to be in a specialist environment where he would receive the support he desperately needed. I needed the statement of education so his options could be broadened. This prompted me to telephone the educational psychologist with regards to chasing up the statement for my son. It had been mentioned at the last meeting but I was not sure if it was being applied for at the end of the Easter term. Surely they had the required six months worth of evidence now in order to make the application? I really felt this needed to be done as I now didn't believe that the chickpea would ever be comfortable in a mainstream class room situation.

Menorca

I have decided to share my experience of going on holiday abroad here for a reason. I often see parents asking about whether they should take their special needs child abroad or simply stay in the country. Not knowing how our children will react to a holiday can be a huge worry. Flying, a different language, the airports and the heat are all factors to consider. The change of routine in itself is a major worry. So here is my take on our holiday abroad.

We went on our jollies on the 17th of May for a week in Menorca.

The chickpea doesn't do excited. He gets upset if we show any excitement too. It's all about the calm. I really found it hard to hold back and not break out with my maraca's and start singing but it would only end up with me being clobbered.

So on day one, we were up at two thirty am in the morning to travel for our six am flight. We treated it like a midnight adventure. This went well. We made it fun with his pillow and blanket in the car and as everywhere was dark and peaceful; our little man was all smiles. I thought it would be a midnight meltdown but he proved us wrong. I suppose I used good tactics. Well done Mother!

We didn't stop on our arrival at the airport either. We had much drama going through customs and passport control. I had gone through with the chickpea and the alarm had gone off. We think it was probably due to the zip on his cardigan being metal. They then needed him to walk through the control point on his own after removing his cardigan but he refused to go without me. In this case they had to frisk him on the other side. For a child with autism this proved a problem. He didn't want to be touched and could not tolerate strangers at the best of times. Now some big hairy, strange bloke in a uniform had to man handle him. I explained to the passport controllers that our son was autistic and no way was he going to let them touch him but they said that the law of the land applied to everyone and he had to be searched. I understood that of course, but it did not help my predicament. I did the only thing I could do and dropped to the floor, took my boy between my legs and bear hugged him while the man searched him carefully. Then taking his hands and stretching his arms out to the side so they could frisk them too. I whispered in his ear all the while that it was OK. My boy was rigid. The man was very sympathetic when he realised how scared the chickpea really was and that this wasn't some kind of crazy cover up, there wasn't a stash of drugs or weapons up the chickpea's t-shirt. It was very awkward and I felt we were being invaded.

Fiasco over and our journey was less fraught after that. We went straight through from the plane to the coach until we reached our destination. The chickpea coped very well with the journey considering.

As he had done so well, when we got to the hotel I decided it was best to go straight for something to eat and then to the pool. I desperately wanted to reward him with some well earned fun. He has always loved the water, in fact unusually so. He is fascinated by it and will play in it for hours, never having shown any fear of it. I gathered this must be a sensory stimulation thing for him.

It was overcast on day two. We didn't know what the heck we were going to do. The chickpea was itching to get in the pool. I don't know how many times I explained to him it was too cold and it was not going to happen today. He just didn't get it. He wasn't bothered that it was too cold. In his head we were on holiday and when you're on holiday you go in the pool. Instead we took him to the kids club and hoped for distraction. I knew there would be no chance of leaving him there but that was fine as long as he was happy. I would be too worried to leave him anyway and as he definitely would not go to a toilet without me or Daddy present it was without question that we would stay with him. He met Esther here, did a bit of colouring and we played connect four with him until lunch time. He remained very quiet throughout. After lunch we walked to the harbour. It had brightened up a little by the late afternoon so a nice walk was in order. The chickpea did not want me to take his photo that afternoon. He hates having them taken. I think it must be because he feels he is not in control. He likes to be the one who takes the photos, maybe being behind the camera is a bit of a mask? It's so frustrating when trying to get a few good family shots. He still wouldn't give up about the swimming pool so we soon headed back and let him have the last hour and a half splashing about.

On Day three it was slightly overcast again. We went to the harbour and had our lunch. Well, the chickpea had lunch. We were going for posh ice creams but he didn't want one of those. He just wanted a chip butty. What kid doesn't want ice cream? Of course, ice cream would be a sensory issue with it being so cold.

We chose a nice looking taverna with two huge obelisks with fire shooting up inside them heating the indoors. I figured they would be a novelty for the little fella and they would attract his attention making it easier to get him inside this 'strange to him' place. I made sure the place was clean too; there would be no way he would go to any toilet in a minging establishment. You need a toilet if your stopping anywhere for food and I always say 'if the toilets are minging then the kitchen probably is too.' The chickpea doesn't like eating in any different or new places so this was a good idea. The chickpea likes his routine but occasionally routine will be broken so you just have to work around it. Always have a back up plan. We had the lushest dishes with various ice creams and lovely toppings while he tucked in to his chip sandwich with great gusto. Autism equals 'keeping it simple.'

Afterwards we walked back to the hotel along part of the Cami de Caville which is basically a bridle path that runs right around the whole island. It was a bit of a walk but the chickpea was an absolute star. He is very interested in nature and looked out for his pet ladybird called Ashanamo. This kept him occupied. Ashanamo is his ladybird. Whenever we see a ladybird anywhere, it is not a different ladybird. It is always Ashanamo, named so by the chickpea. Apparently he follows us where ever we go.

When we got back to our hotel it was a lovely sunny afternoon so we decided it was off to the pool again. The chickpea was desperate to buy a snorkel and goggles with his holiday money so Daddy took him to the shop. I knew they would be a problem for him as soon as he had set eyes on the green snorkel in the shop earlier, but I also knew if we didn't let him buy them we would never hear the end of it. After all it was his pocket money and we had to allow him to make his own choices sometimes. So we let him buy these hulking great green contraptions. What an utter pain they were. It wasn't long before the frustration started to bubble up.

The straps were too tight.

The straps were too loose.

The snorkel wouldn't stay on.

He couldn't get them over his head.

Then when he did get them over his head they fell down to his chin and he couldn't get them back off!

We were heading for a meltdown situation here.

So, quickly thinking I suggested we took them back and swapped them for a lie-low. He had hours of fun in the water with that. It was a close shave but a lie-low saved the day.

On Day four, we went on a boat trip.

The Don Pancho was not leaving Cala n Bosch's harbour until 2 pm in the afternoon so we passed the time by walking for a nose around the shops and having lunch outside in the sun. The chickpea didn't mind the Spanish waiter chatting away to him although he never answered any of his questions. He smiled at him and acknowledged him, but he wont talk to anyone he doesn't know. Heck, he doesn't talk to people he does know. He told me later he liked the Spanish waiter because he was different. I somehow think that the chickpea relates to people who are different as he feels he fits in with them.

Our boat excursion was a three and a half hour trip taking us past eleven stunning beaches and stopping off for an hour and a half at one of them, well that was what was supposed to happen! The beaches truly were amazing and the chickpea could look over the side of the boat through the azure crystal and see all the jelly fish swimming in the water. He was having a great time. I however, felt as sick as a dog!

On the plus side, I had made sure I'd taken plenty of snacks and drinks. I have to say, the chickpea was very well behaved considering the bumpy ride.

When we stopped at Son Saura, a beautiful looking and unspoilt beach, we couldn't wait to get off. I tried to take the chickpea to the boat's onboard toilet before we got off but he was having none of it. I didn't blame him. It was like the black hole of Calcutta. Bleach was obviously a non entity on this Spanish boat and when the engine was turned off, this toilet's flush no longer worked either. I should have guessed he wouldn't go but then I had not envisaged there being no facilities at the beach. Then the captain promptly announces that raw sewage had been washed up on the beach and that was what the awful, rancid smell was that we were turning our noses up to. I couldn't believe what I was hearing. We had forty minutes stranded on a stinky beach and then the boat tried to leave twenty minutes early without us. We hollered and shouted as the captain and his mate were pulling the ropes in. I bounded over the rocks in my flip flops. Look out,

Zola Budd coming through! I felt a bit mean that the boat trip wasn't really what I had thought it was going to be like. It had been a long two and a half hours on the boat and we didn't get the hour and a half on the beach either (not that we would have appreciated it). The chickpea was so good in the midst of this not so wonderful afternoon out. I took him to the beach by our hotel for the remainder of the day to have some fun.

On day five we had a quiet, relaxed morning as we were shattered from yesterday's boat trip. The chickpea just wanted to play pool. He had recently just had a go at playing pool at my friend Sue's house and has quickly developed a liking for it. So off him and Daddy went. He is quite good at it too, once I had explained how to control his cue.

After that he had a game of football with one of the hotel animation team. He laughed and laughed and laughed kicking the ball about and getting Alex to jump about everywhere. Ever since he was a little baby he has always found anything being dropped or balls bouncing, etc, hysterically funny.

After lunch we hired a pedaloe car. This was loads of fun. The chickpea sat on the front like Lord Muckington being driven around. We went down the coast road stopping off at various places for a few photo snaps. One such place was Cap d Artrutz which had a lighthouse. He took some pictures of this. Again, being behind a camera lens holds his attention.

Later in the evening we took a little stroll by the beach to watch the sun going down. We had great fun searching out ants and taking photos of the sunset.

By the middle of the week he was showing signs of agitation. He had two huge meltdowns, one of which was in the middle of Cuitidella which is the city center. I had arranged a bus trip for day six into the city. We were going to have a mooch around the market and view one of the palaces in the city. Cuitedella also has a beautiful harbour which we were going to see because the chickpea loves the boats. We were up, breakfasted and ready for a fun day.

We got the bus to our destination and had to walk through narrow little streets to find the Merkat. This went down well as the fish market was laden with freshly caught fish that morning. The chickpea has a thing about fish so he went camera in hand much to the amused locals. Whenever we go to Asda we HAVE to stop at the fish counter to see the dead fish. He stands there smelling them for ages, obviously sensory input. I'm sure the fishmonger must think were a bit weird!

After that we walked up to a little square that had a windmill with a pub built around it. The chickpea was getting stressed at this point. In his head he must have been feeling very anxious about not knowing where he was. He would have been due for a wee by now too so I thought if I took him in to see the windmill pub this would be fun and detract from any stress. It didn't work! My mistake! He kicked off royally. I had to get him out of there, fighting me as we crossed the road to find somewhere to calm him down. Poor chickpea, to him he was in a strange town with a load of foreign people all talking a foreign language. Blimey, he won't communicate in English most of the time never mind Spanish! He didn't know where he was and just wanted to go home. It was just a total sensory overload for him. I had to sit patiently with him struggling against me on a bench in the centre of the town. Eventually he calmed down. We decided to go for the bus back to the hotel. He wouldn't even entertain the little children's play area which was by the bus station whilst waiting for the bus. It was all just too much.

The last day of our holiday had arrived. I wanted to cram in as much as possible so that the chickpea had a really good day before our early flight the next morning. We went for a walk after our breakfast along the Cami de Caville again but this time the opposite way. We passed lots of coves and the chickpea took pictures of insects along the way. One such was a picture of Ashanamo. We kept walking until we came to a derelict little white house. We had seen this house on the cliff top from the boat on our stinky trip two days before. It was called De Pardals. Just near to it was a white wall and beneath it a stone staircase taking you under the cliffs through a descending tunnel into a cave. The cave had beautiful crystal waters washing into it and you could tell it had once been lived in. This was great topic of discussion for the chickpea who is very interested in cave men, red Indians and Egyptians and basically anyone from history. The chickpea was a little worried if Daddy or I got too close to the edge though and ushered us to stay away. He gets very over anxious if he thinks something is dangerous. In fact he is overtly aware of danger and can over react to things like lighting a candle. He thinks that we will all burn alive!

Our young explorer soon grew tired and he had a good old moan, so we headed back for lunch. This time we had a proper Spanish dish in a little taverna on the beach front. Well I did (fish soup, tomato bread and a glass of sangria), the chickpea, keeping it simple as usual had a burger and chips. He enjoyed lunch with his new soft toy Rabbid which he had just purchased in the local shop. After lunch we settled on the beach again. You just can't go wrong with sand and water - Sensory heaven.

And to end our week we walked for a last look at the harbour, but in the dark to see it all lit up. So all in all our holiday was a good one and I would definitely travel abroad again but maybe there are a few things I would do differently.

Being in Menorca gave me reason to think on a few things. We had gone half board to make life easier. I had been all inclusive a few years ago and I found it to be more than adequate so opting for half board this time round seemed a sensible idea.

When in the hotel restaurant at meal times I scoped around a lot taking in what was happening around us. Meal times were a huge issue for the chickpea. Too many people, too much noise and basically a different routine, not to mention tea being an hour later than we would normally have it at home. These were all factors in a build up to stress. Usually the queues were quite long and I couldn't be bothered waiting. I certainly did not want to drag the chickpea through the hustling bustle of eager people. So I sat back and waited until the queues had died down. I could not believe what I was seeing. No wonder the little guy found it stressful!

There was a heck of a lot of food, plus a lot of greedy people. It looked to me like lots of people with food addictions. Plates piled high with chips and pizza and all the rubbish you can get at home. I remember thinking 'where's your veggies love, your scran is looking a bit bland?'

Food in our diet should be all the colours of the rainbow. There was an abundance of beautiful Technicolour food available, salads and fruit, fresh fish and pasta dishes, gorgeous Spanish tapas. We had the chance to try out what would not normally be available to us so why were these people still eating brown and yellow stodge? There was a lot of waste piled high on plates, especially on kids' plates. Why were the parents allowing such greed? It just made me want to cry. I know I'm no slim Jim but blimey, some of these people really had eating problems!

At the end of it all I was really quite sad. There looked to be so many people needing help, so many people filling the gaps in their lives with food, so many people craving food for comfort. Food makes us feel happy and content and it can become a substitute for something else. We often think of addictions as drugs or alcohol. But it's not just drugs and alcohol. An addiction can be anything. The waste and the greed when so many people are starving elsewhere was quite astounding. I know we go on holiday to relax and enjoy ourselves but this was shockingly wasteful. I decided there and then that I will never go full board or all inclusive again. Not to mention avoiding the pushing and shoving of rude people, mentioning no country in particular.

The Wrong Rainbows

Food is just one kind of rainbow that people will chase. There are many other rainbows that people will chase, and everyone chases rainbows at some point in their life, some good, and some bad. You may not realise it, but we all do it. We all look for things to fill the gaps in our lives or simply, we are chasing our dreams. We all want to feel complete, but to feel complete there are many positives in life that we need in order to feel fulfilled. We all want these things in our lives.

: Love.

: Families.

: Parents.

: Friends.

: A home.

: A garden.

: Parties.

: Children.

: Education.

: Careers.

I could go on and on. All these things and more are essential to our well being. So when we don't have these things we will search for other ways to fill those gaps or replace something that we are lacking. What happens when we can't find the rainbows we are looking for? Why do we need to fill the gaps in our lives? What creates the gaps in our lives? We don't always have love and families and stability in life. We haven't all had stable upbringings. Life brings many complications with it and many rainbows are to be chased.

It all starts from birth. In an ideal world we are born into a loving, caring, nurturing family. We have a Mum and a Dad, maybe brothers and sisters or siblings that follow us. We are warm, well fed and dressed. We have a nice home, maybe a pet to love too. We go to school, make friends, and get educated. We leave school, go on to further education, and get jobs. Then later on we may meet our partners, get married and have children of our own. These are all good rainbows. This is the circle of life. However, it's not usually as simple as this. Life is never perfect.

There are many negatives in life too and to counteract one negative it takes three positives. In relationships the ratio is five positives to counteract one negative. No wonder marriage and partnerships are so hard! They require an extra effort. So what do we do to create a positive or fill a gap? Sometimes our choices can be wrong.

: Alcohol.

: Drugs.

: Affairs.

: Food.

: Bad relationships.

In fact anything in excess can be bad for you. As a rainbow gives us pleasure so can all these things. Like a rainbow with all its beautiful colours we imagine that these things are beautiful and will make us happy, and maybe they do….for a while. We may think that they are positives at the time but they can never have any real long term benefits.

Alcohol for instance is a stimulant. It is a drug. It creates a buzz at the time. Anyone can go out and get smashed at the weekend and forget all their cares. Anyone can let their hair down and live a bit more freely. All their worries go out of the window for a short period. It may be just that one day a week where you can escape.

Escape from the pressure of broken relationships, past hurts, abuse, etc. But what happens when you wake up the next day? Your problems will still remain. What if you decided to drink on a daily basis because you think you can obtain this care free high on a daily basis or just numb the pain on a daily basis. You would then become dependant on alcohol and never really be changing anything. All you would be doing is damage to yourselves. By drinking alcohol on a regular basis we are pouring happy feelings into our system. Our clever bodies then stop producing the natural happy feelings. When the alcohol stops we usually would sink into depression because our happy feelings are now depleted. Our body then needs time to adjust and to realise that it has to start producing its own happy feelings again. It takes time. Long term alcohol abuse can create mood swings, dementia, ulcers, kidney, liver and bladder problems, nerve damage, blurred vision and yellow or blood shot eyes. Well I don't think I would be feeling too ecstatic if that happened to me. So although I chased this rainbow for a while when I was younger, I eventually realised it's not a rainbow with any long lasting happiness and it is not a rainbow I will be chasing anytime soon. Although, what we were going through would have been enough to drive one to drink! It is up to us to discover which rainbows are the right ones and which ones are causing us more harm than good. Which rainbows are the ones that potentially have that pot of gold at the end or which ones will remain covered by the storm clouds?

Drugs are a similar rainbow that people chase. Bit more of a psychedelic one though!

A bit of a Drama

The 10th of June was subject to another review or TAC (team around the child) meeting. I was particularly anxious today. In a previous meeting I had sat and listened to the various agencies arguing amongst themselves about who was to chair the meeting. No one could decide whose job it was to log the minutes of the meeting and they passed the responsibility around to each other. Ten minutes were wasted whilst I sat like Billy nobody in the chair opposite.

Eventually I did pipe up with, "Does it really matter who chairs the meeting? We are here about my son. I don't care who chairs the meeting."

Blimey I'd have chaired it myself if I thought it would have helped.

This meeting was to be just as stressful. It was agreed a letter was to be sent to the LEA highlighting the chickpea's needs and the SCIP was to be updated with the current toileting plans and how the chickpea should walk around the school sensibly as he would often run around without warning. They also wanted to encourage him to begin making relationships with other children and adults although I failed to see how they would do this when he was constantly isolated from the classroom! To add to my stress one of the members of authority at the meeting decided to bombard me with her personal opinion on my blogging about my son. It was nothing to do with the meeting and was her personal opinion. There was me thinking I could help other people with our experiences, and I was being chastised for using a social networking tool to aid other parents with children with special needs. I held myself together very well, holding back the tears and made my point that parents talk about their children all the time on social networking sites, but when she left the room I broke down. I sobbed into my hands with frustration at being belittled in front of a whole room of people. I was doing my best; I was trying to turn a negative into a positive, trying to help my son and do something good. I was humiliated once again.

It was 13th of June. Today's drama would be the onset of my complete loss of faith in this school. I remember the day well as it was my birthday. I will never forget this particular birthday....but for the wrong reasons.

I had dropped the chickpea off at school as usual. I nipped home for my precious hour and forty minutes to myself, squeezing in my coffee before driving back to pick him up. As routine would dictate, I waited in the entrance hall by the main door for him and the TA always brought him over to me. This particular week there was a slight change though. He had been finding using the toilets in school difficult, which was nothing new. The TA was supposed to try and take him at around ten thirty as arranged, and stated on the I.E.P, and then he would have a play outside at break time. If we could get this cracked then he could stay at school a little longer. It was also important for him to have the play time so he could make some friends. He had been doing two hours a day for over six months now and nothing further was progressing. I had explained the toilet routine in the beginning but still no one seemed to get it. I decided that he should be taken to the disabled toilet which was down the corridor, left turn into another corridor and then down at the end of there, instead of the staff toilet which was where I usually waited for him in the main entrance. I always take him to the disabled toilets when we're out, so I figured that maybe this was where they were going wrong. He finds the disabled loo less stressful as there are no people chattering, less noise and the hand dryer does not get turned on which he hates and covers his ears with his hands. In short it is less of a public situation and a sensory overload.

So in view of the new arrangement I would accompany the TA for a few days to make sure the routine was clear and he knew exactly what he needed to do. I walked down the corridor to greet the chickpea.

He asked me "What are you doing here Mummy?"

I got down on his level and explained to him the reason for my being down the corridor. To him I was in the wrong place and so I was out of context. He went in to the toilet and I did my usual tapping on the door to assure him I was still there. I talked the T.A through the routine. It seemed to go well until he came out of the loo. He wasn't happy at all and ran off down the corridor toward the room he would usually have been in at this point. He was having trouble processing this new information. The T.A looked bewildered and didn't make an attempt to go after him. Straight away I knew that this little change had been the trigger.

I immediately thought, 'I need to be where I usually am as he is confused.'

I started off walking back towards the main entrance. I was half way up the corridor when the chickpea came hurtling back down towards us. When he reached me he was growling, hissing and hitting me.

I had to hold him as his arms were flying everywhere, and he shouted to me, "Squeeze me!"

I proceeded to do so. Then from the bottom of the corridor I saw one of the chickpea's teachers come out of a classroom and stomp her way down the length of the corridor towards us. She had a face like thunder and my heart sunk. Oh phooey…what had he done?

She reached me and immediately rained down her temper. I felt like we were being showered with negativity, accusations and a total lack of understanding. I asked could we please not discuss this in front of my son. This kind of thing had gone on in the chickpea's previous school. He had been subject to whisperings whilst he was present, and discussions along with the negative comments. In fact I had asked many times in this school via the communication book, and in meetings for any problems not to be discussed in front of my son as it was damaging to his self confidence. It was also part of his I.E.P and for that very reason. In my opinion it is unprofessional and not good for the child. No wonder his confidence had been destroyed. The kid has hearing like radar! The teacher looked completely horrified that I had dared to ask this.

She said to me, "I want you to come and see what he has done to my room."

I didn't think that this was necessary. Why did I need to go and look at the room? Why did she not listen to me and discuss this in the correct manner?

I replied, "And what do you want me to do with him," nodding down toward my son who was trembling in my arms. It was taking me all my strength to hold him and make him feel secure, I was struggling to pacify him, and she was now demanding I walked back down to a room which could cause me a further problem.

The TA jumped in and said, "I will take him."

It took me all my strength not to produce an eye roll.

So the TA took him in to the hall, and I felt that I had no choice but to go and look at the confounded room. I felt like I was being shamed. She waffled on all the way down the hall how she had been minding her own business and the chickpea had burst in and thrown her work on the floor, kicked her and knocked the chairs over. I listened to her and I felt awful.

Now, fair enough, autism is not an excuse for bad behaviour, but it is a reason. There are still consequences for actions and all children have to be taught this. It's just that our little dears take a bit longer and a bit more support. I got to the door way of the class room and I honestly did struggle to see what he had done. There were two chairs on the floor (easy picked up) and papers scattered on the table. Not a big deal I thought. The teacher proceeded to tell me how the chickpea had come in from no where and kicked her. I did apologise for this as it mustn't have been nice for her. However, she continued to rant on at me until I felt my blood starting to boil. In my head I was thinking 'Hang on; I shouldn't even be in the school right now. I shouldn't be standing here now at all, hanging my head like a naughty school girl. If I hadn't been taking my son to the toilet and doing the school's job for them, then he wouldn't have run off in the first place. And when he ran off surely it was the T.A's job to go and fetch him? I don't really think they allow parents in schools to run around the corridors. Why was I taking the flack for this?'

And then, her last remark of, "I don't appreciate it," tipped me right over the edge.

I jumped in and defended myself and reminded her that I had chosen this school as it had a good reputation for dealing with children with autism. I reminded her that my son has special needs and they were aware of that when he started at the school. I reminded her that my son does things like this when he is stressed out and explained what had just happened and how he was confused that a change had been made. I made a point of how he was only in school for two hours a day and they couldn't even manage that without issue. I had bent over backwards driving back and forth and taking him to the toilet.

I turned to walk away saying "I'm sorry I can't discuss this right now. We will have to do it another time." She had said her piece and I had listened and I had apologised. I had defended myself but I could feel myself about to blow like a bottle of pop. I needed to get out of there. Her ranting was completely uncalled for and unnecessary. It was as if she was deliberately provoking me.

She continued to follow me up the corridor nagging on and on and then I blurted it out, "OH JUST SHUT UP!"

She retorted, "No I won't shut up. Please leave the building."

I spun around and screamed in her face through gritted teeth "I am trying to leave the building."

You could hear a pin drop. She still ordered me to leave the building even though my son was still in the hall. I went in to the hall and fetched him walking out without any intention of ever taking him back there again. The SENCO appeared from another door asking did I want to come in and discuss what had just happened. I was so past it.

"NO" I yelled.

My reasoning had flown out of the window.

When I got home, I cried solid for three hours. My birthday was ruined, but worse still, I had no idea what I was going to do next. I was utterly humiliated. I phoned around the various agencies that were now involved pleading with them to help me, tears streaming down my face asking them what I should do now. I wasn't happy for the chickpea to go back to the school but I also realised I would be cutting my nose off to spite my own face. I needed him to stay there because I needed the school's involvement in order to get the statement. If I pulled him out now I would lose the support and would have to start all over again. I decided that day I was no longer going to aid them anymore. I would no longer make it easy for them by traipsing in and out to take the chickpea to the toilet and doing there job for them. I would make sure he went before we left for school in the morning and if he didn't go in the two hours he was there I was not going to worry about it anymore. Two hours should have been fine as it was not too long a period. Helping them to increase the length of school time was not on my agenda anymore. I would take him to our loo when we arrived back home. I wrote to the school (yet another letter) complaining of the lack of understanding and asked why I was in the firing line when this incident had happened in the school. I reiterated to them that my son was only in school for two hours a day and clearly things were not working out.

I sent him to school as usual the next day with another plan in motion. I set the time on his wobble watch for 10.50am, which had been given to us at Alder Hey children's hospital. He had recently been referred to Alder Hey for bladder training. To be honest the bladder training didn't even get started. At the first appointment, the chickpea was in another new place with another new nurse, all alien to him. The nurse needed him to sit on a special toilet so they could measure how fast his urine was flowing out. I took one look at the toilet and thought 'You have got absolutely no chance of getting him on that contraption.' It was a specialist toilet and he knew it was different.....and I knew that he knew it was different. He sat nicely in the room with me, and he was very well behaved but to try now and get him to do the one thing that was his biggest problem of all, it was like trying to perform a miracle and I didn't have a magic wand stashed down the back of my pants. I tried to get him to go on it by explaining why he needed to go on it, but he became very aggressive which I had predicted. Naturally, I then became stressed because it was just another drama. After much coaxing and not getting very far he then had to be referred to a play worker to get to know him first before they even attempted the bladder training. I went along and tried for several months but I felt it wasn't working for us. We needed to attach electrodes to him in certain places which would eventually be hooked up to a computer so he could play a game. He could then use his muscles which sent a signal through the electrodes to move and guide a fish through a pattern, thus getting him to use the muscles he needed to, in order to control his bladder. The electrodes were just little coloured wires with a sticky tape at one end to attach to the body. He had three wires on his tummy and the other two needed to go where the sun doesn't shine. Needless to say, they had absolutely no chance!

If the watch plan didn't work at school it wasn't a problem, but I thought I would give it a try anyway. The watch is designed to prompt toilet visits, and wobbles rather than rings which may cause distress to the wearer. He got rather confused the first day as an alarm went off on the watch as well as a wobble which he wasn't expecting. The second day he was unsure and the third day he went to the loo. He received a Head Teachers award and a sticker. He went again just once the following week. Although this was a small step it was still progress.

It was decided at last that the application for a statutory assessment would go in front of a panel on the twenty sixth of June. This panel would decide if my son needed a statement of education. Much evidence had now been accumulated and it was thought that the chickpea would need a special school as he was just not integrating into a classroom at all. Even if he had miraculously started going to the loo everyday, it did not solve the problem of his behavioural issues in the classroom. He needed expert support and the right school where they would know exactly what was going on with him and how to approach his needs. Unfortunately, as the six weeks summer holiday were only a few weeks away, and as the assessment takes six weeks, the holidays could possibly interfere with the finalisation date or at worst not be prepared for the panel of experts at all! It would be necessary for me to attend a meeting during the summer holiday with the educational psychologist in order for her to prepare her assessment. I was told it would be mid September before the statutory assessment went in front of a second panel for a final decision to be made. The second panel would then decide with the information provided in the assessments exactly what provision they thought would be best for my child, and whether to actually issue a statement of education at all.

I had to put my trust in these people, people I didn't even know, and it was taking so long to get the support my child desperately needed. I was putting my child's future in the hands of so called experts, hoping and praying for a solution. Hoping and praying that my child would receive what everyone else's children are entitled to. And what is that? It is an education, support, understanding, equality, respect, acceptance, nurturing and the space to grow in their own way. My child is different, and it is OK to be different. Different - not less.

Head teacher

I wrote to the school governor on the 29th April 2013 requesting that my complaint be invoked to stage four. I did not receive a reply until twenty second May in which you wrote you would be arranging this, and would be in touch with me before 7th June 2013.

As you can see from the above date above this is now well overdue and you STILL have not contacted me regarding this. Please do so.

Thank you.

I received a letter from Speech and language in mid June discharging the chickpea from their service as he had progressed and their treatment was complete. Previously they had discovered that the chickpea had no concept of time. He struggled with early and late. This was due to the fact that he takes the 'hands' on the clock literally and it was obviously the cause of his frustration whenever we said things like, 'yes, in a minute,' or 'we will do it later.' What did that actually mean and when is later? He also did not understand negative words like don't and won't. I had been given packs to work through with the chickpea to help him in these areas and they had paid off. With regards to the negative words, the pack was a booklet full of pictures with characters doing things like throwing a ball up in the air. For example, there would be a row of four little boys; the first three showed the boys throwing a ball up in the air and the last one would be standing still. It was my job to ask the chickpea what each character was doing. He would repeat that the first three were throwing the ball up in the air and the last one was standing still. I would then teach him that the last boy was 'not' throwing the ball up in the air thus teaching him the use of the negative word 'not'

The pack for time was a booklet full of little tasks to do like clapping his hands slowly. Each clap is a second and so this taught him the length of a second. And so on through the pack teaching him all about time. He still struggles with time but after his review, Speech and Language felt he had met all the targets. This was good news.

I was proper excited when I heard about the Autism show in Manchester. Who would have thought it, a whole show for autism? I bought my tickets promptly and prepared a picnic the night before. These places cost a fortune for food and let's face it, we all have to eat.

I felt that I was pretty clued up now where the chickpea was concerned. I tend to be the one who knows what is going on with him when he is stressed or I can usually fathom out what his anxieties are about and how to avoid a wobbler, but the more information we had the better. So off we toddled for an autism awareness packed day. I highly recommend it to anyone who can go.

I went with the intention of buying a bear hug jacket or pressure vest. The chickpea loves to be squeezed when he is stressed so I thought he could try it out before we bought one. Unfortunately, the company I wanted wasn't there that day but he did get to try on a weighted fleece and a vest filled with golf balls. I didn't think the one with golf balls sewn into it was very suitable for him. It was a bit bulky and I wanted something that would allow him to feel comfortable as every day use. Walking around like a giant, human sack of marbles may have attracted the wrong sort of attention. Whenever he gets stressed a pressure hug makes him feel secure and has an immediate calming affect on him. This is because the pressure on one area will de-sensitise another area, thus relieving stress.

There was a huge sensory room at the show which the chickpea absolutely loved. It was great to give me ideas.
I thought 'Oh to have the money to kit one of these baby's out.' It was amazing but pricey. There were lots of sensory products too and I came away with a prism ball, a liquid timer and a mini kaleidoscope, plus some fabulous ideas to improve our current sensory room....on a budget of course. The chickpea had a lovely time trying out all the new products on this stall.

There was one stall where I nearly peed myself with excitement when I saw it. It was the flavourless toothpaste one. Flavourless toothpaste I hear you cry! I squealed and danced a jig over to this stall and I couldn't wait to get my hands on a sample for my little man to try. Brushing his teeth has got to be a massive sensory nightmare for him. Toothpaste to him is fizzy and it is too strong, he just can't tolerate it. We were still using milk teeth at this point

140

and he was nearly eight years old, so oranurse toothpaste was a pleasant surprise to find. The chickpea even enjoyed the show immensely. It was tailored on every stall to suit him. The stall holders knew how to talk to him and he was able to try out different equipment. We picked up some good tactics and ideas.

The summer holidays were approaching now and I couldn't wait to spend some quality time with the chickpea. I know he was at home most of the time anyway but the holidays were a good excuse for some fun days out and to take time out of the stressful routine of my being backwards and forwards like a yo-yo to the school, not to mention I might gain a much deserved lie in.

On the last week of term, school held a summer fair. I felt awkward going to the fair after my recent 'bit of a drama' but the chickpea wanted to go, and I felt it was important that he joined in if he wanted to. It was a glorious day and there were many stalls out in the sunshine. I watched my boy as he skirted around the edge of everything avoiding any noisy activities or crowded tables. He played a game of crazy golf and won some sweets playing hook a duck- all games that could be played on his own. I noted that the teacher I'd had the barney with was very nice to me, in fact she fell over herself to speak to me and was ever so polite asking me if I needed anything or could she get me anything. I harboured no ill feeling toward her and I appreciated her kindness. Maybe she was feeling bad after what had happened? Maybe she'd had a bad day and the chickpea booting her had been the last straw? Or maybe she just realized what a tough time I had been having and decided to go easy.

The term ended on a good note. The chickpea's school report was as good as it could be under the circumstances. His teacher reported that which I already knew; that the chickpea had had a challenging year and sadly, he had not been able to make the transition into the classroom.

Breaking through

First there came my own breakthrough. I was so tired and exhausted. My boy had been diagnosed with autism a year ago now and in this last year there were so many things that I had learned.

1. I learned the patience of a Saint.

2. If you want your child's behaviour to change, change your own.

3. To take many deep breathes when my child was explaining something, so much so that I may even hyperventilate.

4. Always let him finish his sentence off, even if I am dying to interrupt. (Hence the deep breathes).

5. Do not bombard him with questions when he comes out of school. He needs chill time after a long day and he can tell me in his own time.

6. Do not ever say 'lets go and jump in the bath or jump in the shower.' I know what I mean but he will take it literally. He WILL jump and jump and jump in the bath or shower.

Saying things like, "Do you want some sponge cake?" are just confusing to him. He thinks I want to give him the sponge I wash the car with to eat. I offered him a slice of hummingbird cake once, to which he replied, "I can't have that, you can't eat hummingbirds!"

Other phrases include, 'pigs might fly,' there was 'blue murder,' it's 'raining cats and dog' and 'pick your feet up.' Just imagine what is going on inside your child's head. The chickpea takes these sayings literally. I still catch my self out saying things like this, its habit, but now I immediately explain them to the chickpea.

7. Turn socks inside out. The seam is less annoying on the outside.

8. I bought a rucksack/back pack and ditched my handbag. I know it's not as glamorous but two hands to deal with a meltdown are so much better than one.

9. I use visual liquid timers or Mr Moo cow egg timer for things like brushing teeth.

10. I used my hand as a clock. My finger tips are morning, knuckles lunchtime and wrist is bedtime. So by moving my other hand across to the relevant zone on my palm I could give him an idea of where in the day we were at, or when things were going to happen.

11. Do not clap, sing or dance….this is a trigger and I may get punched.

12. Do not praise him or clap in an over the top manner. I may be ecstatic but he won't be. This may also result in getting punched.

I had a huge problem trying to implement praise for a long while. It was extremely important to build his trashed confidence up again, but how was I going to do it? It has taken a long time to be able to praise my boy for his achievements. I have had to find a way of doing this without him becoming aggressive and negative about himself. His self confidence had been shattered to a level lower than a snake's belly, where he could not accept any positive thing said to him or about himself. He would insist he was rubbish and hit himself in the face. His self esteem had been slowly destroyed over a period of two years so it was not going to be repaired over night. I learned to give him a thumb's up where due and subtly praise him by whispering a 'well done' ever so quietly. What I really wanted to do was shout from the roof tops like any other excited Mum. I had to take a deep breathe and swallow my bursting pride. Sometimes I felt like I was going to combust with enthusiasm but it was necessary to build his confidence up gradually.

13. I learned many other things too, like creating my own visual bedtime chart and a Birthday chart to give him a countdown of what happens and when. I did these on the computer using bullet points and cute pictures along with each instruction. I did each bullet point in rainbow colour order and laminated them.

14. I also completed the chickpea's sensory room on a budget. Luckily for me having a spare room I was able to do this, but really, even if you have just a corner of a bedroom you can buy a dark den or sensory tent. These are great, but two chairs and a blanket thrown over will do the trick also. It is all about adapting and watching your child closely to see what it is they are trying to show you or tell you. Sometimes they look as if they are doing a really odd thing but nine times out of ten they are doing something for a reason.

Our sensory room is painted in a subtle colour; there are no pictures or anything busy going on in there. We have mirrors on one wall, one of which is an infinity mirror which looks like you are gazing into a tunnel of lights. We have a bubble tube and a colour changing fish tank, a low single mattress which turns into a chair and lots of touchy feely blankets and squishy balls, although my boobs are regularly used as stress balls to the cries of "squishy, squishy." There is a foot spa which is great for calming him and a starlight machine that creates a very realistic starlit night sky. I have also strung some cheap fairy lights around the ceiling. The chickpea tends to like the blue and green lights as they are the calming colours. I learned to use this room as an aid to defusing meltdowns or having story time here.

Looking back over the past few years I had been fighting all this time, in fact I have been fighting my whole life. Fighting to always do the right thing, fighting to make relationships work or trying to fix the ones that have fell apart. Now I was fighting for my boy, fighting for a statement of education, fighting to be heard, fighting for the right school. Something had to give. This was when I put things in to perspective. No longer could I fight for the relationships that were no good for me or were not working anymore. It's all very well me waving a white flag and trying to mend friendships or family feuds but it takes two to tango. It was all very well me writing letters to people and thinking if I sent them I may miraculously fix anything. I couldn't keep chasing these rainbows all by myself anymore, especially when there were more important things to fight for now. Some rainbows are just not meant to be or they fade after time. Many rainbows are absorbing and time consuming and their perfection can detract from what really matters in life. I realised what really mattered in life was my boy and those around me who wanted to be part of our lives. I now had a different circle of friends with whom I connected to and those people who have supported us. I now had a different perspective. It was time to put aside writing letters to people that I now knew I was never going to send. I realised that there was no pot of gold to be had in carrying on with them. It was time to stop chasing relationships that are one sided or not to be. The only rainbow I would be chasing from now on would be for my son.

Another such rainbow I would not be chasing anymore was my beloved Church. I am not saying this was a bad relationship or needed a repair job, far from it. Unfortunately, it was a rainbow I had been chasing that just wasn't working for us anymore. This rainbow had a massive cloud over it and it was hard to see it anymore. I had found that over the last six months the scenario for the chickpea had become increasingly more difficult. When the chickpea was a little tot he would sit on my knee as good as gold throughout the service. I would cuddle him close to me although he often pulled back. He was very quiet, and sitting through the service was relaxed and went without issue. I was not aware of any difficulties back then, even when he used to climb under the chairs and hide. He was easily managed as a babe in arms. As he grew a little older he went into the toddler Sunday school, but he struggled. It took ages to settle him in to a routine but he eventually stayed as the toys were a good distraction. I had mistakenly believed him to be just shy back then. When he was six he was due to transition into the older group but he could not tolerate it. There was too much going on and too much noise and he didn't know any one adult enough to feel comfortable to stay with. They allowed him to stay with the little ones for another year or so but I received mixed messages along the way about whether he was allowed to be there or not which left me feeling confused and not wanting to be a nuisance to anyone. Eventually at seven years old he really was too big to remain with the little ones so I tried to entice him back in to the older group again, but I knew it wasn't going to happen. I sat with him on the sofa but he was socially unable to move away from me and could not join in so I gave up trying.

Often people would say to me, 'Oh it may take him a few weeks to settle' or 'can you just try leaving him and see how he does?' Well there was that idea until they came and fetched me and he was hanging from the door handle with his feet up against the door scaling it like spider man and screaming to get out, or the time he had barricaded himself under the table with the chairs and was hitting out because he was told he couldn't do that! It dawned on me that there was no point in trying to fit a square peg in a round hole. For six months I sat in another room with him so he was happy and comfortable. I would take his colouring pens and books, his leap pad and anything else to keep him occupied in his dinosaur bag. It was a huge mission getting ready for this trip to church every week. The explaining what was happening and at what time. Making sure I didn't forget anything like the juice, the ear defenders and the spare undies. For over an hour, once there I would sit playing with him and try and listen to the service go on at the same time but I couldn't really hear it or I would only get snippets of it. I couldn't take part as I was too anxious waiting and watching for a meltdown or for him to run out of the room. The only concentrating I was able to do was on my child. People were great; some really tried to help me by offering to mind him for a little while so I could go in to the service. I really appreciated this but I still couldn't relax.

Then there was the meltdown when the service ended and he couldn't cope when the room we were in filled up with a large congregation coming in for their teas and coffees. He would attack me out of pure anxiety and I would leave feeling really deflated, always putting a brave face on. Eventually though I had a word with myself. What was I doing? I could be at home with my family instead of having this drama. It was all so frustrating. I didn't want to stop going to my church but all I had done was swapped one battle ground for another. I decided that this was a pressure that I didn't need and I would put it aside for now. From now on I would concentrate on my child and my husband. We were falling apart at the seams and that had to take priority. My church wanted to support me; the trouble was they didn't really know how. And so our isolation grew even bigger.

The most amazing breakthrough happened during the holidays in July. We were at Barnstondale which was an organised summer event for members of Ferries Family groups. Ferries family groups had once again been a pillar of support to me and the one solid thing that did not let me down during this whole fiasco. Barnstondale is a charity run activity centre set in beautiful countryside. They had archery and football, walks in the woods and badge making which the chickpea enjoyed the most.

The chickpea was chatting away to our lovely Elaine who runs the charity when he decided he would wave and say, 'Hello' to her.

I nearly fell over!

I knew he had taken a liking to her but this was amazing. It may seem a very insignificant thing to many people but to me it was a huge breakthrough. The chickpea was seven years old, nearly eight and he had never to that day said hello and waved to anyone. Then he said goodbye too and waved when we left. Thinking about it, I imagined he had never seen the point of saying hello and goodbye, after all why say goodbye, when you will see that person again? Maybe he saw goodbye as something final? He also never says night-night at bed time either. Maybe he had just clicked with these social greetings. Autistic kids miss social cues but somehow this cue had all of a sudden dawned on him. He still has difficulty with hello and goodbye but he will say it to people he knows well, or maybe, just maybe you will just get a Chewbacca noise. Who knows?

I decided at the weekend to go to a church with my daughter in Liverpool. She attended a different church to me and I was really missing my own church. I wanted to be close to my daughter after a personal family problem so I tagged along with her. I didn't expect for one second that the chickpea would go in to a new place without issue so I was totally gob-smacked that he then went in to the Sunday school with my daughter and she came out leaving him in there.

I mouthed over to her in the midst of a noisy congregation, "Where is he?"

She gestured behind her and I panicked thinking, Oh blimey where is he? I had a picture of him in my head running amok and having a meltdown because he wouldn't know where he was or who all these strange people were. She then gave me a thumb's up letting me know he was OK and I became quite overwhelmed.

He stayed in there for the whole session colouring and interacting with the kids workers. This was a huge achievement as he had never really gone in to any Sunday school before and stayed willingly. He asked me when we were going back to this new place. We went back again the following week just in case the week before had been a fluke. He stayed in the whole session again. The team here was really clued up on autism and had got straight down on the chickpea's level. He loved it. Needless to say we wanted to back again and I decided to give this new church a trial period over the summer holidays. I was aware this could be just a honeymoon period and anything could happen. I wouldn't get my hopes up; it could just be for a season.

We had two bone dry weeks at this time and the chickpea seemed to be more relaxed using public loos. Probably the golden stars we were giving him worth a whole pound were helping. Bribery can get you everywhere. Also the fact that he wasn't in school which was very demanding of him, allowed him to relax a bit.

One summer morning the chickpea told me he'd had a dream the night before.
He told me God was talking to him again and telling him to 'just ride.'

He said, "I know what that means."

Lo and behold, (I had totally forgotten about the dream by now) he came back from the park with his Dad and he had learned to ride his bike in the space of half an hour. I was so proud of my boy. He'd had trouble in the past balancing and keeping steady but today he did it. He was eight and had really struggled with this milestone so we were extra pleased with him.

He came in and said to me "Now I know God is real."

This little boy who has had so much to deal with in his eight years and he truly believes in God. He trusted and he did something amazing. So all in all, I really felt that we were starting to see several breakthroughs.

Around this time I received a reply regarding the complaint to school 1. In order to proceed to stage four without delay, the governor now needed a lot more information from me which made things increasingly difficult. I had to prepare paperwork to present my complaints to the chosen committee, and forward them to the school before the hearing. I was asked to provide the names of the staff that had helped me through my social networking page, and the letter suggested that my complaint was against them personally. This was never the case; it was the case that if the school had not been failing my son, this method of contact would never have even been considered. I was required to provide full private conversations from my social network account and the names of staff who had not agreed with the decision to exclude my son from the school trip; also the name of the person who had discussed my private letter was requested. I had to think hard about this from a Christian point of view, and from my view as a parent of a child with special needs. How was I going to marry these views together? I wanted peace but also to be heard on my son's behalf.

At the end of July the chickpea had a routine visit to his paediatrician. The paediatrician recorded how he had been only managing two hours a day at his present school, and spending this time in a separate class with the teaching assistant as he was unable to access the classroom environment. She noted my concerns at the time regarding the chickpea's sensory issues. He enjoyed certain sensations on his feet and had difficulty with clothing, shoes and labels. He struggled with textures and tastes of various foods and usually smelled the food before even considering eating it. He also liked to smell me. She noted that I had said how he bounced and jumped around and would deliberately bang his head on the bed over and over in order to achieve a certain sensation. He would also lie upside down with his legs up the wall and he responded very well to being squeezed tightly, I had invested in a pressure vest to aid this. At other times the chickpea could not tolerate being touched at all. Taking all this in to consideration the chickpea was referred to the occupational therapist for a sensory assessment. She was sure that we would benefit from their support in this area. I took this as another minor breakthrough in that we were going to get some help around this issue.

She also noted at the time, that we were due to visit the kidney specialist for a follow up appointment. The chickpea's recent kidney scan had been in August and was pretty much the same as the previous one showing an enlarged kidney, which was to be expected as it is doing all the work of two kidneys. The chickpea remained on medication due to another recent further infection of the urinary tract.

In September the chickpea had an amazing first week back to school. Given the changes of going into a new year, a different classroom and a different teacher he coped fantastically well. I was so very proud of him. My feeling was that the summer break had done him the world of good. His confidence had increased dramatically in these few short weeks. He had established some new friendships and some good coping strategies. One example of this was, knowing when he needed to use his ear defenders or spotting the meltdown signs in advance and being able to tell us. On his first week back to school he had managed some time in the actual classroom. This would be such a small thing to anyone else but for us it was another huge step. He managed fifteen minutes on the first day and twenty five minutes on the second day. He also completed a spelling test. I had to roar with laughter though when he brought this piece of work out at home time to show me. His TA told me that the chickpea's task that morning was to tell a story in pictures. He said that he had decided to draw a poem that his Dad had taught him in pictures. So I looked at the pictures and this was written along side.

The sun was out.
The sky was blue.

Down the road,
the poo cart flew.
The wheel fell off,
a scream was heard.
A man was killed by a flying turd!

At the end of the week he came out to me with another surprise.
He had received a special praise award. This was an amazing
achievement for our boy. This didn't mean that all of a sudden he
could cope. Realistically this was just a period of two hours a day
over the first week back. Again I was aware that this would be just
a honeymoon period and as soon as the pressure was applied he
would be likely to blow.

As predicted he had a huge meltdown on the Friday night. There
was a copious amount of screaming and confusion which was
obviously a build up of stress and over stimulation from the
whole week. The poor little guy's birthday was also looming which
was a huge issue for him and he had been worrying about that on
top of going back to school.

As birthday's go, this year I had a plan, I had to approach this
occasion with a different mind set. I was not going to make a fuss
and organise any party. It was always too much for him to cope
with. This year I opted for going to good old MacDonald's. He
could choose seven friends to invite thus keeping the numbers of
children to a minimum. I would buy them all a happy meal. So in
that case the toy was provided with the meal and no need for
party bags. There were balloons available at MacDonald's if the
children wanted one. I popped a lollypop in each happy meal and
bought them all an ice-cream afterwards. I took the cake along
and cut everyone a piece but refrained from singing the dreaded
tune which would more than likely send my son under the nearest
table. It was the cheapest and best birthday he had ever had.
Paying attention to what our child actually needed instead of

going along with what we presume to be normal or traditional really paid off.

I stopped thinking he was missing out if we didn't sing happy birthday to him, and thinking he was missing out because he wanted to sit in a corner quietly and not join in with whatever was going on. If that was what he wanted to do then who are we to say he was missing out? Tradition is something that people do that they have always done, because they like it or they are used to those routines. People like to follow a pattern because it makes them feel comfortable. The trouble is what is a comfortable routine or tradition for one person doesn't mean it is comfortable for someone else, namely the chickpea. In that case I decided from then on we would make our own traditions and patterns. We don't have to do what is expected or what we think is normal, we would go with our instinct and change the traditions and routines making our own up.

The statement

On the 1st of October I picked my son up from school at eleven o clock as usual and things had not gone too well. It was only Monday, the beginning of the week. I was ushered in to a classroom and his new class teacher began relaying to me an incident that had occurred that morning regarding the chickpea being restrained. It seems my son had been very stressed indeed. He had been running around the school and hitting himself. They decided to restrain him as in their opinion he could have injured himself or someone else. She proceeded to show me exactly how my son had been held down by herself and the TA, by the shoulder and arms. They both sat either side of him with one hand gripping his shoulder firmly applying pressure and their other hand holding his arm lower down. They also each wrapped one of their legs around one of his legs so he physically could not move. In other words they acted as a human straight jacket! I did not absorb the entirety of what they had done to him until I got home later and thought about it.

On leaving school my son told me he had not wanted to be touched and he was also hungry. He said that his T.A had changed the rules and he could not have his snack until after he had done his work. This was the trigger point. Surely the T.A knew change was an issue? Surely he knew how hunger can be physically painful for any child with autism? As the chickpea has sensory issues this would most definitely have caused a problem. The chickpea also said that he was hitting himself and drinking his juice in order to make himself cry. He thought if he cried then no one would touch him. He was trying to find a safe space, hence running off by way of finding this.

My son told me the T.A would often say, "Go on then, run off!"

My son would not have understood the T.A's sarcasm and taken his words literally. As he was then prevented from running off, it would have caused immense confusion and then the meltdown which resulted in him being restrained on this occasion. As much as I liked his T.A I had to finally admit that he lacked experience in the autism department. It was no wonder to me that the chickpea could not cope more than two hours a day. My head was pounding all the way home.

What my biggest issue here was, that on changing my son when I got home I straight away noticed the dirty great red hand print mark on his left shoulder.

Horrified, I immediately asked him "What the heck is this?"

It dawned on me before he had even answered my question and my blood started boiling. The force that must have been used was excessive for the incident in my opinion. There were two finger marks and two thumb marks along with three lines of broken capillaries where three fingers had squeezed and pinched his skin tightly. While I understood the need for restraint on occasion, I found this utterly unacceptable and far too excessive. I reached for the phone with my boy sobbing at my feet. Once again my heart broke for him. He had been confused and humiliated.

"I'm sorry Mummy, I'm sorry."

I assured him, "You have not done anything wrong son. Nobody is allowed to touch you and hurt you like that."

"I didn't want them to touch me."

"I know," I said.

With fumbling fingers I dialled parent partnership for support and to report the incident to them. On their advice I immediately emailed my concerns to the school and attached a photograph of my son's arm and informed them that I wished to see the schools physical intervention policies. In the meantime I decided I would be keeping my son at home with me until this incident was rectified. I was not going to allow him to be put in this position again. As it was, the chickpea would have been off the following Thursday as we were going to look at another school that specialised in autism. Really, I didn't even see the point in him going back to his present school for the sake of two hours a day which had not progressed any further since the beginning of the year. I felt as if even the teachers couldn't be bothered making the effort now. They knew that if and when the statement came through that he would be transferred to another school. They knew he would be moving on. It was as if it didn't matter anymore and they could just give up on him.

I was informed by email that my concerns would be passed on to the Deputy Head teacher. I received a second email the next day from the Head teacher saying that she had not been in school when the incident occurred. She told me she would contact me as soon as possible to let me know how the concerns I had raised would be dealt with. I would wait a further fifty one days for a reply before needing to consult them again regarding this matter.

Unbelievably, at the same time as this incident had occurred (as if I could handle much more,) I received the proposed paperwork in the post for the hearing for four out of the five complaints which I had at school 1. After careful consideration I had opted to continue with my complaint without providing the names of staff and the conversations from my social network site that I had mentioned. I felt that all that would be achieved in providing this evidence would be those members of staff being penalised and they were the very people who had actually helped me. They were the ones who understood the need for that one to one contact, and that information being passed on to each other was vital. I certainly did not want them to get in to trouble for communicating with me. I wanted the school to except that no one would have contacted me out of school hours if they themselves had done so in the first place. I wanted the school to recognise that mistakes had been made on their behalf and to learn from them. I wanted them to take responsibility for their failure to provide my son with an education and above all failure to provide for his extra needs. What I wanted most was empathy and an apology and to prevent what happened to my son happening to another child in the future.

In the case of my private letter being discussed I opted to speak to that person directly as I felt that it was a better way to resolve this part of my complaint. I had considered that person a friend and did not want to get them into trouble, but this issue certainly needed addressing. I was unsure about the friendship and confused over it but I came to the conclusion that I would still be a friend to her anyway, even if it was not reciprocated. I had now rendered my fifth complaint of breach of confidentiality non applicable and I dealt with it myself.

With regards to the rest of the complaints, I had previously in July, painstakingly filled in a separate form for each issue. The complaints fell into three different categories including;

1: Exclusion from a school activity.

2: Adequate level of care for medical needs.

3: Support provided for special needs education.

I was required to list each one which I did very carefully after having kept all correspondence over the last few years. Keeping any correspondence in matters like this is essential and very much advised. I was then able to provide detailed information including dates, times, letters from doctors and paediatricians to aid my complaints. I then had to write out and fill in information under the headings 'Action already taken to resolve complaint and response,' and again under a second heading, 'Actions I feel may resolve the problem at this stage.' Needless to say I'd had a lot of writing to contend with and that alone could have filled another chapter. So now in front of me was the completed paperwork I had filled in along with school's proposed responses and adjustments and a date for the hearing - which I could not attend! Yet again there was another delay; I just wanted this over with. I wrote back requesting a new date and submitting all the forms.

A few days after the restraining incident, I went to view the special school that had been named as being able to supply provision for the chickpea. I was excited and anxious all at the same time. This school had a brand new unit with a sensory area. They had small classes with an expert teacher in autism of thirteen years. It would be perfect given my son's sensory seeking nature and the need to be in a calming environment. My excitement would be short lived!

I arrived at the school with the chickpea in tow, obviously as he had been removed from his current school pending their action. We were greeted by what would be his class teacher, a lovely lady who had a tranquil aura about her. We were then joined by the head teacher who proceeded to shake my hand. Her demeanour appeared to be stern and unwelcoming which made me more nervous than I already was.

She looked me up and down and said, "You do know that this does not guarantee him a place here? This is only a look around today. We will need to assess your son in the school setting."

I was dismayed to say the least and replied, "He is not in school at the moment."

"Well, when he is back at school, we will need to assess him then."

I explained I had taken him out of the school for the time being due to being injured whilst being restrained and I wasn't sure when he would be going back in.

She almost spat at me, "Well we restrain here and if you don't like it then this school is not for you."

I felt the necessity to defend what I was trying to say. I was not saying I disagreed with restraining but merely stating it should be carried out in a safe manner that does not injure the child. I understood that on occasion it was necessary to perform a restraint. She was very prickly with me and it set me on edge. The class teacher then took me to her classroom. I entered the room to find several children as still as statues in their seats. It was very quiet and eerie for a school setting. I was showed to the back of the classroom where the sensory room adjoined and was available if the need arose. The chickpea went in but he found it hard to leave my side. The teacher was very assuring and I felt that under her wing the chickpea would progress but it niggled me about the way we had just been treated.

Five days later a package dropped on my doorstep. I hurriedly ripped the brown paper open to reveal the proposed statement. I knew it was on its way (hence viewing the new school which had been suggested in it) but to have it in my hand at last was a victory. A surge of relief washed from my head to my feet and once again the floodgates opened. I scanned over the document unable to absorb its content properly through the blinding moisture and mascara that was running down my cheeks. I was relieved briefly. This victory was dashed with the news that my son was refused the place at the new school we had just visited.

It had been a tough week, what with the chickpea being restrained on the Monday, visiting a school that made me feel awkward on the Thursday and then being told he could not have the place there after all. After my initial excitement at us finally getting this statement, I was now wondering why I had fought so hard for the last eighteen months. What was the point of this legal document when there was no provision anywhere for our son, or where there was provision it was refused? I had spoken to the statementing officer over the phone who told me there were no places for him anywhere in ANY schools. The only one place that had been available for him was in a school that seemingly was expert in the autistic area and yet they had refused him entry without so much as assessing him. They had made this decision entirely on the paperwork alone. I was told that as the school's unit for children with autism was new, they wanted it to be plain sailing and successful.....so my son was not being given this resource just in case he was not manageable and he caused disruption. They did not want him upsetting their perfect new unit even though this very unit had been created for children just like him who so badly needed it. Where was the sense in this and where did that leave my boy now?

The statement was later confirmed in November.

Nothing is Impossible

I was then given a choice of two schools; neither that I liked the sound of. The first school being a good distance away and although he would be entitled to transport, I felt the journey to and from this school would be too much for him to cope with. The school apparently was a hard one to get a place at but it somehow didn't feel right. The second school I had heard had a reputation as a 'naughty boy's school' so my immediate reaction was, 'I'm not sending my son there.' I was in a predicament, what was I going to do? I wondered again about the point of the statement and thought to myself why God would allow me to come this far and then not have a suitable school for my son. I knew I had to trust him that he had this covered. If my child can trust God to ride a bike then he wasn't about to let him down with the wrong school. I remembered a verse from the bible.

Proverbs 3:6, 7

Trust in the Lord with all your heart and lean not on your own understanding; in all your ways submit to him, and he will make your paths straight.

I decided, who was I to judge whether a school is a 'naughty boy's school' or not. Who is anyone to say a child is naughty anyway? I couldn't listen to what others were saying; I needed to find out for myself. There were plenty of people that had called my son naughty because they didn't understand. Quite plainly it is ignorance. I phoned the head teacher to make an appointment. I expressed my concerns to him over the phone. He reiterated just what I had been thinking anyway, that no one has the right to judge until they have seen for themselves. He seemed very pleasant, assuring me of how hard the teaching staff work at this school to support children with difficulties, and he invited me along to see the school.

I went along to the school taking the chickpea with me. I arrived at reception feeling rather nervous. I explained I had an appointment to view the school and the lady buzzed the door open to let me through to a waiting area. I sat down and listened intently to the children in the assembly hall next door singing. This school appeared normal enough so far. I waited ten minutes or so before another lady came through the door from the hall in which the children were singing.

She said to me, "Hello, are you here to look at the school?"

I replied, "Yes."

What she said to me next blew me away and things could not have been made any clearer to me.

"Someone will be with you shortly to show you around. We have just been having our school assembly in the hall about Nothing is Impossible."

I burst in to tears and I knew what I knew what I knew. It was too much of a coincidence to be a coincidence. I held my face in my hot hands, knowing that God really, really, really did have it covered.

The poor woman must have thought I was some kind of fruit and nut cake. I couldn't have explained this for one second when she asked me, 'are you OK?'

All I could say was, "I know my son is coming here."

I viewed all the classrooms and the teachers were all very welcoming, pupils seemed happy and content. I spoke to the head teacher in his office and he demonstrated on my son how they restrain at this school, who just sat there and let him do this with great ease. My mind was made up.

So the big day was set for 28th October, after the half term holiday. Obviously I wasn't going to make a fuss by telling him it was a big day - that would be a huge mistake. To make a fuss would make him anxious and stress him out. All I told him was that he was starting his new school on Monday morning. As he had been to see it with me he knew where he was going. I told him he would be going on the school bus so he had time to absorb what would happen on the morning, but without getting over excitable about it.

His uniform was ready and labelled. His PE kit was ready. I didn't tell him it was a PE kit though. I just said it was just shorts and T shirt. Sometimes the wording of things can create a barrier and given that the chickpea had never ever done PE in either school 1 or school 2, I thought it was a good idea to just say shorts and T-shirt. He probably associated the words 'PE kit' with a noisy hall and children running around creating a total sensory overload for him, therefore him not putting the kit on rendered him disallowed to join in as a school rule. This was his solution for avoiding that situation. So if I were to say the words PE kit, I would have created a barrier straight away.

My husband couldn't work out one time why the chickpea didn't want to go and help him fix bikes in the shed with him....until he worded it differently. Instead of saying 'Come and help me fix bikes' he rephrased and said, "here you go son, can you hold my spanner for me?" He received a completely different response. The wording 'fix bikes,' must have made the chickpea feel like he had to fix the bike. He knew it would be too big a job for him, so he used tactics to avoid feeling like he has failed or would fail at something. He will avoid a situation he feels he won't cope with by any means. This is called P.D.A which sometimes goes hand in hand with autism.

The chickpea was going from a two hour day to a full school day. This was going to be huge for him. Play times and lunch times, toilet times and the dreaded 'W' word - work. New faces, new teachers, new sounds, new classroom, not knowing where he is or what is expected of him, new uniform, and change of routine.

A lot of people said at the time, "can't he be graduated in?"

To be honest I think this had been a mistake in the past. By easing him in gradually he got used to doing just two hours a day, therefore when a change came to extend the time he couldn't cope with it. So full days it was. We would ride out the storm and hopefully we would come through the other side to a bright and shiny day. I had no idea how long the storm would last but it was inevitable in my mind. I was thankful for our sensory room. I could see it being put to very good use in those coming weeks.

So, the day arrived for the chickpea to start his new school. I had his uniform all ready, his butties in his box, his bag packed, shorts and T-shirt. This was going to be a big step and I prayed to God he used the toilet there.

We were ready at eight am as requested by the transport company. We sat patiently. He seemed fine. He seemed to have absorbed what was happening today and was not anxious at all. It does help when he is clear about what order things will happen.
Fifty minutes later it was me who was the anxious one, I felt sick! The bus had still not arrived. I phoned the company only to find they had gone to the wrong address. I couldn't believe it. Why hadn't they phoned me? Apparently the house they went to was empty so it wasn't as if they thought I was just not answering, or we were still in bed, they must have known the address they went to was wrong. I was so upset. I had wanted today to run as smoothly as possible with no hitches, hitches that can cause melt downs. I had waited so long and fought so hard and I just didn't need this and neither did the chickpea. It seemed to be one hurdle after another.

I made a swift decision, I could sit and worry about it and pick on all the negatives, or I could do something about it to avoid the stress. I was learning to always have a back up plan. I grabbed my car keys and I took him to school myself, and he went in with no problems.

Through the day my chest kept tightening. I felt dreadful and I was a total bag of nerves. I phoned the school and the lady I wanted to speak to was on her lunch break. I phoned back half an hour later and she still wasn't there. A few minutes later, thankfully she called me and reported that the chickpea was fine. He came home that afternoon with a huge beaming smile on his face and showed me his little certificate with 100 points. He had joined in PE putting his pumps on (which had not happened in over two years) and played bingo. Amazing!

The chickpea then completed two full weeks, with lunches, going to the toilet and coming home each day that first week with 100 points bar one day when he got a cool 98. He made a friend which hadn't happened at all at his previous school. He joined in theraplay which he loved and he brought work home to show me. ACTUAL WORK! He also completed set homework.

I was well aware that this was a 'honeymoon period' and when he had settled things could change. I would have been daft to think from then on it will be all hunky dory. He is autistic and there will be challenging times ahead no matter what or where he is. Every day brings a different dilemma and a different issue. Everyday I am in defuse mode.

I waited for 'The phone call,' to tell me there had been an incident, it did not occur.

Meanwhile some things still needed closure

The Replies

The date of the hearing arrived just three days after the chickpea had started at school 3. It was as if everything was starting to come together and I would be able to find peace of mind soon. I had my prepared, accumulated documents with me in a rather large bundle. They were all in chronological order marked with post it notes where I felt it would be necessary to speak out. I had high-lighted any other relevant parts. I was not nervous in the slightest, I had waited for this day for so long, waited for the chance to put my points forward and speak out for my boy because he had been unable to. There had been several times over the last eighteen months when I had asked myself was it worth carrying this on? I was so tired and the whole thing had been soul destroying, should I just forget about it and move on? The chickpea had left school 1 so long ago now. What would I actually be achieving? I simply felt that I had to see this through for the sake of any other child with special needs passing through this school. But then, what of all the other mainstream schools that this happens in? My child is not the first and he certainly won't be the last. We had been through almost three years of hell, and now, here I was, at the pinnacle of my complaint. Elaine from Ferries Family groups accompanied me as my friend and my support.

I became quite emotional when I got to the school. I now understood why my son shook and palpitated at the mere mention of it. As I walked through the car park towards the school entrance I became overwhelmed. The spot where my boy had collapsed in a gelatinous heap, leapt out at me like a sore thumb. The window where I had looked through to see my boy's flushed red cheeks and his sad, hollow eyes because he was so ill and he couldn't tell anyone - thus it had gone unnoticed, the path to the classroom door where I had stood in isolation feeling weary and down trodden. Those emotions welled up in me again like a fountain of hot bubbles. And this was a reminder of why I was here. I gathered myself together and after having a word with myself and a prayer from Elaine, I moved on to chase this rainbow.

I entered the classroom that had been prepared for the appeal, to a panel of three governors sitting at a table opposite where I and the head teacher would be sitting along with our representatives. They all introduced themselves and outlined the format of the meeting. I was allowed to commence the meeting by stating why we were at this stage, what my complaints were, and what I wanted the outcome to be. For over an hour I went through each complaint carefully one at a time, reading out what I had written and emphasising my concerns. The head teacher's representative was allowed to respond to each complaint and I in turn was allowed to explain further why I was not satisfied with their response. I kept my composure throughout and remained firm and clear. I was determined not to break down. When all of my complaints had been addressed and discussed I was then asked if I would like to add anything further. Was this a trick question? Too right I did!

I felt I needed to look at the head teacher face to face and tell her exactly how I felt. I had not dragged myself through all of this because I had a bee in my bonnet. I hadn't put myself and her through this for the fun of it. This was serious for me but I also wanted her to know that I am a forgiving person and that my heart was a loving one and not one full of malice or bitterness.

I turned to face her and said this, "I chose this school because it has a Christian ethos and I want my son to grow up knowing Jesus. I chose this school because it is two minutes away from our home. I tried and tried for a very long time to keep my son here and make things right. The last thing I wanted to do was to remove him from a school he had been in since he was two years old but I felt I had no choice. Why else would I remove him from the school if I wasn't so desperate? I had to take my little boy away from the only two friends he had in the world and everyday he tells me he misses them. It breaks my heart. All I want for you to do is admit that you made mistakes and then they can be put right, everyone makes mistakes, we are all human and it's OK. At this point the tears came, however, I felt she needed to see some emotion and for her to know what this situation had done to us as a family. Sadly, she refused to turn her head and would not even look at me.

At the close of the meeting she left the room and each one of the panel came and spoke to me. They all asked how my son was doing now and they took a genuine interest. I was so relieved it was all over and thankful that the people who were on the panel showed some compassion.

Eleven days later I received my long awaited reply from the complaints appeal. I had hoped, but it was no surprise to me that not one of my complaints were upheld. Their reasons, they found no evidence to support my claims. Clearly I hadn't moaned enough! The letter was a repetitive compilation of previous responses from the school. They stood by everything they had already said and were in agreement with how my son's needs and support had been approached, including the decision to not inform the T.A that the chickpea had autism, and the exclusion of the school trip. They did however express regret that the situation could have been managed differently. If I had complained at every given opportunity then it could have been a different outcome. Through my appeal, the school made a decision to introduce a written record of incoming calls of such incidents to improve communication internally. It was agreed that communication on the whole should be looked into. The head teacher also expressed regrets that there may have been a lack of communication in supplying all relevant information to the supply teaching assistant. The panel wished to apologise for this. The panel were however very insistent that I was made aware that the school had used their own school budget to provide for our son's extra needs. As he was not statemented at the point when the extra needs arose, he would not have been entitled to government funded support. Surely the school didn't begrudge using the school budget for something that was as necessary as this? I felt as if it was begrudged given the fact that it was mentioned at all. I was confused by the letter; it was as if it contradicted itself. There was a refusal to accept the mistakes made, but on the other hand a lot of regrets expressed and the panel wishing to apologise for them. I was angry at first, and feeling as if the whole thing had been a waste of time but I read over it again. Instead of picking out the negative points I homed in on the offer to resolve the complaints. There was the decision to improve communication by logging and documenting all calls, there was also an acknowledgement that they should have employed a teaching assistant who was experienced in autism spectrum disorder rather than someone (who as lovely as she was) only resembled his aunty. I had achieved something here, but not only that, whatever this letter said, I had faced the school in that meeting and told them how I felt. I spoke up for my boy because he couldn't. I fought for my child and no one can ever take that away from me. Whatever the outcome, I knew I had been heard. At the end of the day, despite the school's best efforts, my child had suffered emotionally, his confidence had been destroyed, he had contracted UTI's due to being left in his own mess, and he was let down. Why else would I remove him from the school? But, it was time to put this palaver behind me. I would move on and learn to forgive. It was over!

I wish to complain.

I am concerned as I have still not heard anything about the incident that occurred at school with my son fifty one days ago. I find it hard to believe that a child can sustain an injury and still nothing has been done about it by the twenty first of November. I have emailed you on two occasions but I have not had a satisfactory reply.

As already stated the SENCO had told me exactly what had happened on the day, and how she had restrained my son. I am also concerned that the TA was not 'team teach' trained in order to do this? On arriving home and changing my son's clothes I straight away noticed the marks and asked him about it. He told me 'it was the lady' (being the SENCO). The marks were consistent with her description of the restraint and on the side that she had held him. You will also see from my photo that the time of the photo will match up with the time scale and date of the restraint. Can you please update me about my concerns? If I do not have a satisfactory outcome I will take this matter further.

Thank you.

As I felt my complaint regarding the restraint at school 2 had fallen on deaf ears, I contacted the safe guarding officer during these fifty one days. I could not believe I had found myself in a predicament in which I needed to escalate things once more. Had we not been through enough? Had my child not suffered enough? He had now been injured and seemed to amount to no importance to anyone in authority. The safe guarding officer contacted me and directed me back to the school for an update of my complaint. I acted as directed and the school told me they would contact me shortly. Were they for real? Two months after the incident had occurred and I still had no acknowledgement of what had happened, let alone an apology. I told them that I just wanted a satisfactory reply and for the SENCO to admit she had made a mistake. I told them this needn't be a huge issue but I was left hanging like a carrot dangling in front of a donkey. I had to ask myself now, was it really worth going through this whole charade again? Could I put myself and my family through the turmoil and stress of yet another complaint and seeing it through all the stages? Could I again commence the long and drawn out process of formality to be heard on my child's behalf?

On 12th December I eventually received a reply but it was not what I had expected. School 2 reiterated back to me that the chickpea had been running around the school and they regretted the restraint but it had been necessary. They said it was necessary in order to prevent him hurting himself or others around him. I already knew this and understood that but I was staggered when they suggested that he had caused the said injury to himself. Seriously, did they think he had landed one dirty great upside down hand print on himself complete with broken capillaries? They referred to the photograph I had sent them and said the local authority designated officer had formed the opinion that the marks were consistent with a child who was running around and hitting himself. I was livid. The hand print was double the size of his own hand, and the wrong way round for him to have self

174

inflicted it…and they knew it. It was ridiculous to suggest. The SENCO knew what she had done and this was blatantly covering up her mistake. I knew she would never have meant to be so heavy handed and purposely injure him, but to use this excuse was beyond belief. Although I had the evidence to prove my point and I could have taken this matter further, I decided that given the length of time it took for my complaint against school 1 to be heard, and the outcome, it just wasn't worth it. I would leave it to the conscience of those involved. It was time for us to move on and live our lives. I could not allow myself to become consumed with this. Our lives had been on hold for long enough.

Unfortunately, school complaints procedures are far too long and drawn out, leaving parents exasperated.

The Pot of Gold

And so, moving on, I cannot believe the progress that the chickpea made over the first year. It was hard for me to trust the new school in the beginning because of the promises and let downs that had gone before. I waited for the dreaded 'phone call' for months, for me to go and get him or he had kicked off, still in fear every time it rang. It never did.

This school has a point system which is broken down in to tens. Each child can gain up to one hundred points a day for good behaviour. If a child gets one hundred points in a day he receives a little certificate with his achievement on it, thus rewarding them visually. If he gets one hundred points every day for a week, he gets a bigger certificate with five hundred points achievement on it and a red badge meaning they can access options as a reward. If they consistently receive five hundred points a week they can achieve a prize at the end of the school year for the most red badges. There are also other colour badges for lower points than one hundred so no child ever feels that they have underachieved and have in fact made progress. They receive certificates for keeping their cool, best lunchtime behaviour and any other achievements. I now have boxes full of these.

During this first year he caught up enough to be graded just below average. Given the fact that he had not even been able to be graded before, and had fallen way behind, this was amazing. I could only imagine what the next year would bring. His reading and writing are fantastic, he even writes short stories and poems (takes after his Mum). He is very artistic and his potential there is being realised. Confidence wise, the damage that had been done had been over a long period of time so I didn't expect it was going to be fixed over night. However, I am happy to say that this school has worked wonders for the chickpea's confidence and his self esteem. They have worked with him as an individual creating a personal profile with his likes and dislikes, needs and special needs. The classes are much smaller and there are one to one teachers so the children have constant support. In this school they listen to the parents but they also follow through what has been agreed upon. They communicate with us and they totally 'get' our kids. There is a parents group each week where I have found some lovely friends and much valued support. I could not do without them now. These parents have been on a similar journey to me. I have heard stories of how a small five year old was restrained by virtually six teachers on top of him, stories of children taking years to be diagnosed and years to get through the system to access support for special needs. By the time we had all got to this school none of us could take anymore.

Various courses are run each week for us allowing us to access outside support and give our children the very best that we can. This school knows that by supporting the parent, they are supporting the child. This new school was nothing short of fantastic.

Some of the chickpea's achievements to date are;

: Doing P.E in full P.E kit.

: Doing set homework.

: Sitting in the school assembly hall.

: He had a speaking part in his school assembly. (We all cried).

: Taking part in the nativity play. (We all cried again).

: He achieved the most red badges in his class for the whole school year. (More crying).

: Taking part in his school fairs.

: Not one single accident......Not one!

: He is now on the school council.

The storm I had expected relating to this new school never ever materialised, and has not done so in over two years. Instead, we have found our pot of gold at the end of the rainbow. I now have a happy, confident and much brighter young man. This is not to say that life is a bed of roses, far from it, but where school is concerned the structure and routine are vital to our son's happiness and well being

This just shows that with the right support, the right people and the right attitudes that our children can and will cope. My child is not a 'different' child now, he is the child he is supposed to be, he is the child he was born to be, he is being nurtured and built up. He is learning and thriving in an environment that suits his needs. He is just like a prism refracting white light, positivity is now being invested through him and now his colours are shining out, reflecting his true persona.

It took two and a half years to get here, out of which an eighteen month battle for the statement we so desperately required, but this rainbow was worth the chase. It has been a long, tiring and hard journey but the destination is second to none. At last our child has what EVERY child is entitled to, acceptance, understanding and an education.

A new day has come!

Luke 1:37

For with God nothing shall be impossible

Index of Abbreviations

ADHD - Attention deficit disorder

ASD - Autistic spectrum disorder

CA - Carers allowance

CAF - Common assessment framework

DLA - disability living allowance

GDD - global development delay

IEP - Individual education plan

IHCP - Individual health care plan

IPSEA – Independent parental special education advice

LEA - Local education authority

ODD – Oppositional defiance disorder

PDA - Pathological demand avoidance

PIP - Personal independence payment

PUV - Posterior urethral valves

SCIP - Social and communication individual plan

SEN - Special education needs

SENCO - Special education needs coordinating officer

SEND - Special education needs and disability

SPD - Sensory processing disorder

TA - Teaching assistant

TAC - Team around the child

UTI - Urethral Tract infection

Other books by this author

From Care to Somewhere